D0711236

Parenting With Love
WITHOUT ANGER
OR STRESS

by
Bob Lancer

Parenting Solutions
Marietta, GA

Bob Lancer's

Parenting With Love
WITHOUT ANGER OR STRESS

Second Pringing: 1999
Third Printing: 2001
Fourth Printing: 2003
ISBN 0962866652

Published By:
Parenting Solutions
P.O. Box 70031
Marietta, GA
30007
(770) 592-8100

*For a free catalogue of additional books, special reports, audio tapes and video tapes
of Bob Lancer's work, For more information about Bob Lancer's Parenting With Love
Seminars, To schedule Bob Lancer for a speaking engagement
send your request to the publisher or visit:
WWW.BOBLANCER.COM*

I lovingly dedicate this book to my parents,
without whom it would not have been written
and to my child, whom it's all for.

★

"Kinship is a question of spirit and not of blood. How often
do we find persons, who, in feeling, are absolutely strangers to
their own brothers and sisters! Occaisionally even parents fail to
understand their children… Later, this same child may evolve
aspirations and ambitions that seem to the other members
of the family mere whims and vagaries…" Elbert Hubbard

Acknowledgements:

First, I wish to thank Richard Heiman for your inspirational contribution and your wonderful cover design, Joan and Ray Robbins for introducing me to Sir Richard and for your wonderful beach at A Highlands House (my bed & breakfast retreat on the Panhandle) – and Ray for your generous sharing of business wisdom, Nina Lacey for your editing that taught me to write less passively (not that time), the experts I have interviewed on my radio show who teach, confirm and help me to clarify, every parent, teacher and child I have had the privilege to serve: you teach me as much as I teach you, and the pioneering work of those teachers who gave me breakthrough lessons, including and especially: Dr. Maria Montessori, Dr. Alice Miller, Isidore Friedman, Ralph DeBitt, Alfred Korzybski, Dr. Wayne Dyer, the classical authors too numerous to list and Bob Dylan, soul brother and spiritual awakener - may _yooh_ stay fahrevah yuung!

Parenting With Love
Table of Contents

◆

"Come mothers and fathers throughout the land
And don't criticize what you can't understand
Your sons and your daughters are beyond your
command..."

Bob Dylan

Introduction

"Take Charge Now!"

This book teaches you how to be in charge in your relationship with your child. When I say, "be in charge," I do not mean dominating your child. Essentially, this book shows the parents of all children, including the parents of children diagnosed with A.D.D. and A.D.H.D. and the parents of so-called "strong-willed" children, how to discipline with love, peace, power, and poise.

There is no trick to child discipline. In the real world of your moment-to-moment experience, the child discipline process goes beyond systems and methods. No rules exist to follow mechanically.

However, you can replace your frustration and impatience when parenting with greater composure. You can guide your child's behavior and support her development without losing your temper, screaming, nagging, pleading, or hitting. You can end your child's disrespect, whining, arguing, bossiness, manipulation, non-compliance, tantrums, and ugly sibling rivalries. This book shows you how.

This book presents what I believe to be the key to success in parenting: how to parent more consciously. As you parent more consciously, you discover a way of parenting that truly works for *you*, and you begin recognizing what your child needs from you to feel good about herself and to behave beautifully.

In the pages that follow, you will learn how you can transform typical, every-day "trouble spots," such as bedtime, mealtime, homework, and leaving punctually in the morning into continually more smoothly-flowing, stress-free routines.

You will learn how you can handle the every-day challenges of parenting with less aggravation and more calm and competence every single day.

Your child came into your life to help *you* grow. Your dedication to continually moving toward your own highest potential is what it takes to be more successful with your child. The more "strong-willed," manipulative, testy, uncontrollable, or domineering your child, the more you need to develop wise and loving self-control and self-knowledge to adeptly handle that child.

Recently, the Atlanta affiliate of NBC did a special report on my child discipline workshop, which is called "Take Charge Now!" The newsperson referred to me as, "The guru of parent temper control." I teach parents that taking charge of their children begins with taking charge of themselves. One of the major lessons of my workshop, and of this book, focuses on how to *take charge of your own behavior* to bring out better behavior in and to create a more sacred, loving and fulfilling relationship with your child.

The first part of this book primarily deals with the start to child discipline: parent self-discipline. In it you will learn how to take charge of yourself to improve the results you are getting with your child.

The second part of the book focuses on the factors that shape the development of your child's behavior. It teaches you how to avoid contributing to the behavior you want your child to stop exhibiting and how to provide your child with the influences she needs to behave in the loving, responsible manner you want for her.

The third part of the book teaches you simple child-discipline methods, or how to respond to the behavior you *do not* want so you can create the results you *do* want. These methods provide you with a parenting methodology that addresses your child's natural need for parental firmness. You will learn, for example, how to administer consequences, which do not include screaming or hitting, to teach your child accountability and to help him behave within respectful boundaries.

The fourth part of the book provides you with simple, tested "parenting solutions" to every-day child discipline problems faced by virtually every parent. These "recipes" for producing the outcomes you want with your child focus on such specific challenges as bedtime, mealtime, lying, and sibling rivalry. You also will find basic guidelines for dealing with issues relating to single parenting, step-parenting, divorce, and relating with your spouse in ways that meet your child's needs.

While you may believe you have a child-discipline problem, the experiences you have and the results you achieve with your child accurately portray how *you* function. As you exercise better self-control and practice being more alertly aware of what is going on with yourself and your child in the present moment, you will function in new ways that produce better results.

◆

Parenting With Love

Parenting with love is about parenting
from trust instead of fear,
from love instead of anger,
from strength instead of weakness,
from peace instead of stress,
from balance instead of strain,
from patience instead of rush,
from awareness instead of unconsciousness,
from intelligent self-discipline instead of
automatic habitual reaction,
from understanding, respect and kindness,
with an absolute commitment
to enjoying every sacred moment
you have with your child.

◆

PART I

WHERE TAKING CHARGE WITH LOVE BEGINS

◆

1

Parenting With Peace, Poise and Power

Taking charge with your child begins with taking charge of yourself *first*. When your child's behavior "makes" you react with anger or stress, he demonstrates that *he* really is the one in charge. When you respond to your child's demands in an overly-submissive or overly-stern manner, or when you react with anger to your child's disturbing behavior, you feel, and to some extent you actually are, out of control of yourself. You, in turn, feel like the victim of your child's behavior.

The way out of this "parent victimhood" begins with self-control. Your child will stop trying to control you with poor or disturbing behavior when her efforts to do so fail to work. This happens when your reactions to her behavior change. As long as she can get you to give-in to her excessive or disrespectful demands, cause you to react with anger or stress, lure you into nagging, pleading, arguing, screaming, or hitting in a desperate attempt to gain control, she places you in a dependent position. You allow yourself to be placed there, and, in the process, you lose control.

The more you strain to control your child, the more out of control your child likely becomes. When you lose your peace and poise, you lose the power to direct yourself and your child. Practice parenting with peace and poise, which means making your first priority your own emotional balance and self-control.

A Way To Improve Your Future Self-Control

Make a list of the ways your child behaves that trigger your loss of peace and poise. Perhaps it happens when she cries and nothing you do soothes or quiets her. Perhaps it happens when she whines. Perhaps it happens when she stalls instead of getting ready for bed, tells you that she hates you or disregards your directions after you have told her repeatedly what you want her to do. Perhaps it happens when she behaves poorly in public.

Writing this list serves as a way of increasing your awareness of exactly when you lose your peace and poise. This helps you to exercise more self-control the next time a similar event occurs.

When And How To Take Control

The practice of peace and poise does not mean that you remain passive regardless of how your child behaves. It simply means that whatever action you take is firmly established on a base of peace and poise.

There will be times when it takes all your strength to remain calm. There will be times when you do not have the strength to control your child and maintain your emotional balance at the same time. In such cases, you may have to let your child do as he pleases. Of course, if your child engages in truly dangerous behavior, do what you must do. You do not need a book to tell you to react without concern for your peace or poise if your child walks toward an oncoming train.

However, sometimes a child will do - or nearly do - dangerous things to get you to react. If it works, he will go on overstepping his bounds and placing you in the position of having to rescue him from himself. Wait and watch for as long as possible. Give him the chance to take responsibility for himself before taking responsibility for him.

You cannot always be in perfect control of your child or yourself. However, as you practice maintaining your peace and poise, it will become easier for you effectively to direct your reactions to your child's actions

We used to believe that reacting to a child with anger caused the child to improve her behavior. Now we know that an angry reaction may be exactly what the child wants to elicit. The child will continue doing whatever makes you react with anger or with feelings of powerlessness and victimhood as long as you continue to react in that manner.

Monitor Your Feelings

Notice your feelings every moment. When you feel nervous, stressed, angry, impatient, or insecure around your child, concentrate on recapturing your peace and poise. Work directly on "centering" yourself, or maintaining a sense of peace, relaxation and security in response to whatever is happening. Center yourself by taking a moment to observe the way you feel. Think of how you want to feel. When you begin to feel peaceful and poised, you are centered and ready to deal with your child and the situation at hand.

Stop Blaming

To lose your anger you have to stop blaming your child for *making* you angry. Your anger represents *your* reaction to your child's behavior; you have the ability to *choose* a different reaction.

When you notice yourself feeling angry or frustrated, stop thinking about your child's behavior and focus on your own. Regard your angry or stressful reaction as the *first* behavioral problem with which you must deal.

The Key To Accurate Judgment

When you lose your peace and poise, your judgment becomes impaired. Anger and stress distort your ability to decide upon an adequate response to the situation. You cannot accurately judge what is happening, or what is best to do when you lack peace and poise.

When you believe you have to handle a problem with your child immediately or to take absolute control right now, you lose your peace and poise. Thus, rushing into a decision affects your judgment. You do not have to rush into a decision. You can take your time.

A parent in my workshop related a story about her child throwing a tantrum in the supermarket. She became upset and wanted to teach him then and there never to repeat this behavior. She caused herself unnecessary emotional stress by expecting to accomplish so much so quickly. To begin changing his behavior and taking control, she need only have demonstrated for her child that his tantrums had no effect upon her. All children have tantrums for the same reason: to gain control. If you react to your child's tantrum with emotional disturbance of your own, your child's tactic has worked.

You may not be able to improve immediately your child's behavior forever, no matter how severe the consequence you impose. So, let the first consequence you impose be the consequence of your peace and poise. Before you attempt to aggressively control your child's behavior, liberate yourself from being controlled by it. He may employ a particular form of misbehavior again and again until it finally sinks in that it is not getting him anywhere. When he realizes you are not reacting stressfully, he also will realize he has lost control of you and that your emotional state is dependent upon him no longer.

You can determine the most productive response to your child's behavior from your peace and poise. When you are calm and emotionally centered, you possess the most clear and reliable judgment. You can see, sense and know the exact procedure to follow to achieve the results you truly want with your child.

Your Peace Radiates

One of the greatest aspects of peace and poise is that they "radiate." Your emotional states radiate from you and influence all around you. As you center yourself, the people with whom you come in contact receive your centering influence. Children calm down and demonstrate happier, more respectful and cooperative behavior in response to the peace and poise of the adults around them.

Practicing peace and poise around hyperactive children proves especially necessary and beneficial. The more hyperactive, angry, jumpy, aggressive, or disorderly your child's behavior, the more challenging it becomes to maintain your peace, but it can be done. By holding your center of peace and poise, you automatically assist your child in calming down.

Essentially, your power to remain centered and to maintain your peace and poise must grow stronger than your child's power to disturb your emotional state. The stronger your peace and poise, the more centered, orderly and harmonious your experience of and your influence upon your child.

Daily Exercise

Your ability to maintain your peace and poise grows like the strength of any muscle. Exercise it regularly. Practice handling every parenting problem with peace and poise and without anger or stress. Do this by remembering to make being centered your constant, daily objective. On an index card, or on the back of an old business card, draw the following triad-symbol of parent power:

Power

Peace   Poise

Carry this diagram around with you throughout the day. Look at it often. Keep it in mind so you remember to concentrate on maintaining loving peace and poise with your child at all times. Every day, build the habit of reducing, and finally, eliminating any anger, stress and impatience in your reaction to you child's actions.

Losing your habitual angry and stressed response in your relationship with your child may be the greatest challenge you ever assume. However, this may also be the most important challenge because you cannot teach your child better self-control while losing yours.

It Is Better Not To Be A Bomb

Parents sometimes ask, "Is it better to have a long fuse or a short fuse?" I tell them, "It's better not to be a bomb at all." Wherever your exploding point, your child will find it.

When you lose your peace and poise, you lose your power. It is that simple. Practice handling everything to do with your child a little more calmly and patiently, and everything will become easier to handle. When your child refuses to go to bed or dawdles when you need to leave, do not strain and stress yourself by reacting with intense anger in the moment. Anger will not help you gain control; it will help you lose it. The instant you grow angry and tense, your child responds with his own angry opposition.

Your practice of peace and poise in and of itself creates more peace, love and harmony and reduces conflicts or power-struggles in your relationship with your child. Your peace, poise and power serve as the foundation for parenting with love.

◆

2

A Better Way To Win With Your Child

"Insanity is doing the same thing and
expecting different results."
Ancient Chinese Proverb

After I introduce the peace-poise-power approach to parenting at my child discipline workshop, often a parent will query, "Bob, I understand the need for peace and poise and how much better it is to respond that way, *but how am I to get my child to do as I say?"*

I typically respond with my own question: "What have you been doing up until now to achieve the compliance you want?"

"I have tried everything," comes the common reply.

"Please be more specific," I request. "Look back and think of exactly what you did the last time you wanted compliance and did not get it."

The parent thinks for a moment, then says, "Okay, now what?"

"How well did that work?" I ask. "What were the results of your actions?"

"What I did didn't work at all," replies the parent. "That's why I'm here."

My answer: "Then stop doing what does not work and try something different."

This may sound glib, but my answer points to a crucial factor in finding a better way to win with your child. When you do not like the results you achieve, instead of blaming your child and getting frustrated, accept that you need to find and apply another way. A better way to win with your child does exist, but you cannot find it as long as you continue repeating responses that produce disappointing results.

Increasing Your Parenting Power

Your parenting power increases when you focus upon what *you* do to create the results you achieve with your child. When you achieve the desired results, how have *you* behaved? When you have not achieved the desired results, how have you behaved? When your child does not comply with your direction or request, how do you react? Take a good look at your reaction and at its affects upon yourself and upon your child. Does it achieve the results you truly want?

Becoming more conscious of your behaviors and reactions in relationship to your child frees and empowers you to find a better way to relate to him. You have the power to create different results, but you lose that power when you do not use it and resort instead to habitual parenting behaviors.

Typically, when children defy parents, the parents feel frustrated and humiliated and end up repeating themselves, nagging, pleading, arguing, demanding, losing their temper, screaming, or hitting. These prove to be painful and costly ways of attempting to gain control of the situation and of the child. Even if one of these responses does achieve compliance, the parents find no satisfaction in that result, because they still feel the stress and strain of how they achieved it.

How To Find A Better Way

Achieving your child's compliance and cooperation requires that you use *conscious* trial and error to find the way that works best. If your child ignores your requests or directions, obviously merely making requests or giving directions is insufficient for producing the results you want. You may have to time your requests better or make your directions more explicit.   You may have to back up your words with consequences. Perhaps the way you have been reacting to your child's non-compliance has taught her that she actually has more to gain by defying than by complying. It also may be that you have overlooked some of your child's needs, making her poor behavior a natural, logical response to the treatment she receives.   You may need to address those needs to get compliance.

One parent recently complained that for the last 10 years she *"had to"* check her child's toothbrush every night to make sure he had brushed his teeth. Imagine that. In 10 years she has not come up with a better, more dignified way of dealing with this issue.

Coming up with a better way does not require much effort. You simply have to look at what you currently do and consider your options. Sooner or later, a better option will occur. All of civilization has advanced in this manner, and your parenting will do the same.

Choose A Better Way

Maybe you feel you do not have any other choices. It can seem that your child "makes" you angry, "makes" you repeat yourself, "makes" you raise your voice. As long as you consciously or unconsciously believe that your child's behavior or demands force you to respond in demeaning and fruitless ways, your belief makes that your reality. Then, you really do not have any other options.

However, no one in his right mind would *choose* to lose his temper or become stressed. No matter what you currently do to achieve your objectives with your child, remember: better options exist. Accept this fact, and you are on your way to discovering better and better parenting options. Do not forget that *you choose* the way in which you react, and other choices always exist.

You *Do* Have A Choice

When you think about it , you really do not have to yell when your child does not listen to you. If your child ignores you when you speak in your normal voice, you have the power *not* to raise your voice. You do not *have* to feel humiliated, frustrated or embarrassed when your child behaves improperly in public.

When you *automatically and habitually* react to your child's behavior, you really do not have a choice. Automatic, habitual, mechanical reaction patterns steal our freedom of choice from us. If you do not pay close attention to *yourself* you will react in pointless, strained ways that lead to increasing frustration and disappointment.

As long as your habitual, automatic, angry reaction patterns dictate your feelings, actions, speech, and thoughts, you do not have the freedom to choose to parent with more peace, poise and effectiveness. Your freedom to choose a better way of parenting begins with first recognizing your habitual response patterns and then...Choose The Right Response.

◆

3

Choosing The Right Response

Before you do something about your child's behavior, it helps immeasurably to know *what* to do. You do not want to just do *something*. You want to do the *right thing*. You want to do what *works*.

Your reactions produce consequences. Therefore, the manner in which you react to your child's behavior determines the results you achieve. Your parenting power lies in your power to choose your reaction to your child's actions.

Typically, when children behave in an annoying or troublesome manner, the parents become so focused on the children or on the problem posed by the children's behavior that they pay no attention to their own reaction. Hasty, automatic, emotional reactions represent the primary obstacles to choosing effective responses.

Teaching Manipulation

Let us look at an example that demonstrates the importance of choosing the right response and how difficult that can be.

Few things pain parents more than seeing their children unhappy; however, parents must carefully watch how they respond to their children's apparent gloom. If your child discovers that he can seize control of your heart strings by exhibiting sadness, he may deliberately demonstrate unhappiness for effect.

Children fall into manipulative patterns such as this one unconsciously without even realizing they behave as they do to achieve a specific result. Yet, because children do tend to adopt unconscious manipulative behaviors, it becomes all the more important for parents to be conscious of their reactions to those behaviors, to become the masters of their reactions to their children's actions. Also, just as your child can unintentionally use manipulative tactics to control you, you can respond to your child's behavior in ways that unintentionally set you up to be manipulated by him.

Teaching Testing

Examine how you respond when your child tests your limits to her behavior. When she again and again does what you do not want her to do, thus challenging you to react, notice your reaction. If, for example, your child's behavior annoys you, annoyance becomes what you contribute to the situation. However, feeling annoyed does nothing to help you or your child.

In fact, when you react with a show of annoyance toward your child's behavior, you may give your child exactly what she wants, thus encouraging her to repeat the tactic. Children often behave poorly on purpose to gain attention or control. By giving your child what she wants, you make it more likely that she will continue and repeat the behavior. Thus, your annoyance actually may produce the opposite of your desired outcome.

Look At Your Reaction

The way you react to your child's behavior demonstrates your way of handling that behavior. Your reactions bring you peace or stress, anger or contentment, sorrow or joy, love or hate. Your reactions, not your child's behavior, bring you these feelings. The way you react produces the outcome you achieve.

For example, if your child says to you, "You're mean! You hate me!" look at your reaction. Statements like these trigger feelings of guilt in most parents. Can you control your reaction to your child's manipulative use of words, or do you react purely in response to the feelings your child's behavior elicited within you? If you cannot control your reaction, your child has found a way to control you and you cannot control the results your reaction produces.

How To Make Change F.A.S.T.

Your awareness of your reactions, and of the results you achieve through your reactions, increase your freedom and power to respond differently for different results. Therefore, awareness leads to control.

Look at this example: When you repeat your child's name over and over again in an attempt to get his attention, what do you accomplish? How do you feel when *you* behave this way? When you study the dynamics of such an encounter you see the futility of your reaction to his inattention, and you can then choose a better reaction. As you read previously, a better way always exists.

Practice being aware of your *feelings* (F), *actions* (A), *speech* (S) and *thoughts* (T). I call this the formula for making change F.A.S.T. Paying attention to these four aspects of your interactions with your child increases your self-awareness. And when you do so, you automatically find better ways to use these elements in your relationship with your child.

The diagrams below illustrate how your actions and reactions influence the outcomes you achieve with your child.

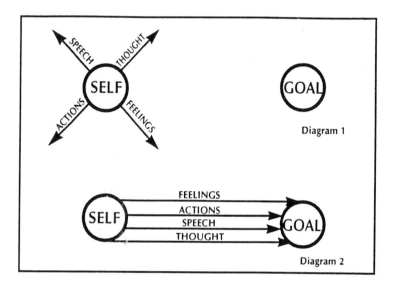

The circle with the word "goal" inside represents what you want to achieve. For instance, you want to achieve your child's compliance without a battle, with peace and poise. To achieve this objective, you have to apply your feelings, actions, speech, and thoughts in such a manner that they fall in line with that objective.

Diagram 1 illustrates what happens when your reactions are out of control. Although you want to achieve an objective, your thoughts, speech, emotional reactions (feelings), and physical actions do not advance you in that direction. No matter how fiercely you react, your objective remains separate from you.

Diagram 2 illustrates the more effective response choice. Your feelings, actions, speech, and thoughts work in line with the outcome you intend to produce.

Make Slight Adjustments

Achieving desired results with your child depends upon how you handle the four elements of the F.A.S.T. change formula. You can look back at any frustrating experience you have had with your child and see how you misapplied one or more of these elements. Perhaps when your child cried in the night your emotional reaction (F) was needlessly strong. Perhaps you allowed yourself to run into her room to rescue her too hastily (A). Perhaps you lost control of your speech (S) and repeated yourself in a mechanical, thoughtless manner or lashed out critically complaining, "Why must you always..." Perhaps your thoughts (T) were so focused on your child's behavior that your anger and frustration grew until you had no mental space left to think about a more effective response.

You can always make adjustments in your application of these four elements *to some degree* to bring them into better alignment relative to what you want to accomplish. By bringing your feelings, actions, speech, and thoughts in line with your goals, you gradually improve the effectiveness of your actions and reactions, which allows you to more quickly and easily produce the outcome you truly want with your child.

Watch Your Focus

Focusing on how you handle your child's behavior empowers you to release your automatic, emotional reaction habits. The next time you feel frustrated by your child's behavior, repeatedly ask yourself: "How am I handling this situation? How can I handle it differently?" This question helps you regain your self-control. By taking the time to question your reaction, you take the time to get centered so you can choose a response that will work.

The next time your siblings bicker, for example, avoid getting so caught up in their behavior that you forget to focus on your handling of it. Regard your reactions as your way of dealing with the situation. Observe the effects of your reactions upon yourself, your children and the situation. If your reaction increases your stress and strain, drop it and choose another. If your reaction increases the intensity and frequency of your children's quarreling, drop it and find another. Patiently focus on choosing the right response instead of automatically reacting with criticism, anger or stress.

Responsibility Equals Power

In a very real sense, responsibility equals power. You give your power to direct your life to *whomever* you make responsible for what happens to you. In this case, when you blame your child for the anger, stress, nagging, pleading, or arguing in which *you* engage, you give your *child* the power to *make* you respond in these ways.

You empower yourself to improve your responses for better results when *you accept complete and total responsibility* for the way you react to your child's behavior. Your reaction to your child's behavior equates to what you do about your child's behavior. Giving your child responsibility for what you do gives your child the power to control you. In contrast, taking responsibility for what you do in relationship to your child gives you the power you need to parent effectively.

◆

4

Conscious Parenting

The use of one particular key practice will help you achieve the best possible results in your relationship with your child. This practice, called *Conscious Parenting*, entails paying close attention to yourself, your child and the relationship between the two of you. If you do nothing else but practice Conscious Parenting, you will find your own way to better parenting with love.

By becoming a more conscious parent -- and please read this *consciously* -- virtually every one of your frustrations passes away as you discover easier, more loving and satisfying ways of relating with your child and bringing out your child's best.

The Law Of Three

Everything you say, think, feel, and do in your relationship with your child affects three essential factors: you, your child and the quality of the relationship between the two of you.

You cannot create a peaceful, loving relationship with your child by accident. You can, however, do so purposefully. Since your actions and reactions affect you, your child and the quality of the relationship between the two of you, you must take control of the way you impact those factors. If you do not, the quality of your relationship with your child will, in all likelihood, distress you both.

The individual who introduced me to the importance of these three fundamental elements of all relationships referred to them as "The Law of Three." As it pertains to the parent-child relationship, this law can be diagrammed in this way:

RELATIONSHIP

PARENT   CHILD

How To Apply The Law Of Three

To apply The Law of Three means paying attention to your actions and reactions as well as to your child and to the relationship between the two of you. No matter how bad things have gotten between you and your child, you can create the kind of relationship you want by focusing more alert attention on these three factors.

The quality of your relationship with your child does not depend solely upon you, but you can produce the best results possible only by doing your very best. Practicing Conscious Parenting by focusing specifically on the factors involved in The Law of Three, automatically clarifies new and superior options for winning with your child

Unconscious Parenting

Unconscious Parenting represents the opposite of Conscious Parenting. Since Conscious Parenting means paying attention to The Law of Three, Unconscious Parenting means ignoring your impact upon yourself, your child and the relationship between the two of you. For instance, when you lose your temper, yell, nag, plead, hit, criticize, endlessly repeat yourself, waste your energy on pointless explanations or unnecessary arguing you demonstrate Unconscious Parenting. When you engage in these kinds of behavior you abuse yourself, you make your child angry, unhappy and hostile and you increase the discord and conflict between yourself and your child.

Unconscious Parenting means using blind, automatic reactions to your child's actions. Instead of paying close attention to the affects of your behavior upon yourself, your child and the relationship between the two, you react habitually, impulsively and automatically, and then you angrily criticize and blame your child for how *he* behaves.

Unconscious Parenting is like unconscious driving. Without awareness of the effects of your driving, you cannot drive responsibly. When you alertly recognize how your driving affects those around you, you can make choices and take more responsible actions.

Your automatic, habitual ways of living and relating may not work with your child. The more you complain about your child's behavior, the less responsibility you take for your own. By practicing Conscious Parenting, you instantly begin recognizing how you contribute to the problems you have with your child, and new and better ways of dealing with your child's behavior become clear. You will find that you *always* can improve the results you have with your child simply by paying closer attention to what takes place between the two of you.

Conscious Parenting In Action

Six-year-old Jonathan was playing with a friend. His mother, Sue, decided to check on them and witnessed her son kicking the other little boy. She screamed angrily at her child and sent him to his room. Humiliated and frustrated, Jonathan stomped upstairs and slammed the door shut. He then opened it to scream out, "I hate you, Mom! I don't love you anymore!"

In this situation, as in all others, the practice of Conscious Parenting could have helped Sue every step of the way. When she saw her child kick the other little boy, she could have first observed her emotion before letting it dictate her action. Recognizing that she was upset, she could have chosen *not* to take any action for a moment.

By paying close attention to what happens when you react in anger you discover that anger increases resentment and rebelliousness in your child. By just observing your feelings without allowing them to drive your thoughts, speech or actions, the wave of emotion soon passes without causing damage.

Had Sue allowed her anger to pass in this way, she then could have looked at the situation calmly and considered an appropriate response under the circumstances. One such response might have been to calmly walk over to her child and, without embarrassing him, take him aside. Then, she could have firmly said, "Kicking and hitting are against the rules. If you do that again, your friend will have to leave." This clear, unemotional message, delivered with respect for the child's feelings and concern for maintaining good feelings between herself and her child, could have produced better results.

When You Do Not Know What To Do

Do not demand that you always instantly know what to do about a situation. When you do not know what to do, just pay attention. You rarely *have* to react quickly. True patience means trusting in the time it takes to intelligently respond. Calmly, patiently observe. Something will occur to you.

Conscious Parenting offers one immediate benefit. Since your behavior patterns radiate and affect your child, just calmly watching -- rather than emotionally reacting -- has a settling affect upon your child and assists him in being more aware of his own actions.

Responding Responsibly

You teach your child responsibility by responding responsibly. Responding responsibly means applying the Law of Three instead of automatically and emotionally reacting without concern for the impact of your reactions.

For most of us, applying the Law of Three requires having the intention to do so, because few of us are in the habit of paying much attention to what happens in the present moment. We just react. It takes a special effort to remain conscious of the three essential elements of your relationship with your child -- you, your child and the relationship between the two of you -- especially when you are emotional, tired, rushed, busy, thinking, or speaking. The effort to parent more consciously, however, will prove to be the most worthwhile effort you can make.

◆

5

The G.A.T.E. Of Self-Control

Since *your* behavior determines the results you create with your child, gaining conscious control of your reactions becomes paramount in creating the kind of relationship you want with your child.

In this chapter, the last in Part I, I will present the four basic laws that govern your ability to maintain calm and loving self-control while parenting. Function counter to these laws and you will find it virtually impossible to avoid angry, frustrating reactions to your child's natural behavior. Heed these laws, and it becomes increasingly easy to maintain your peaceful, poised, wise and loving power in your relationship with your child. I refer to these laws as "The **G.A.T.E.** of Self-Control."

"G" Stands For <u>G</u>rowth By Small Degrees

With regular exercise, self-control **Grows** like the strength of a muscle. By consistently disciplining yourself to practice maintaining your peace, joy, patience, trust, and love, even under the most challenging circumstances, your ability to maintain these powerful, positive states grows by degrees. Although it may be difficult to believe right now, your persistent practice of emotional balance and tranquillity eventually makes peace and poise your automatic, habitual way of parenting.

To strengthen the power of your wise and loving self-control, the next time you feel tempted to react with anger and stress, do not do it. To whatever degree possible, consciously and intentionally maintain your peace and poise instead. Each time you exercise your power to maintain your peace and poise, your power to do so **Grows** by small degrees.

"A" Stands For <u>A</u>wareness

Practice being more **<u>A</u>ware** during your interactions with your child. Begin to observe more alertly what takes place between the two of you in the present moment. When you function with awareness, you free yourself from past automatic reaction patterns. You see your reaction to your child's actions as it happens. When you are fully present in the moment you are less likely to react as you have in the past. You will notice what you do to create your own frustrations as well as your current opportunities for achieving more positive outcomes.

Every day offers you the opportunity for parent education. The next time a problem occurs between you and your child, give yourself some time to look back at what happened. Look at how your child behaved and look at how you handled that behavior. Then, ask yourself, "What can I learn from this? How could I handle something like this a little better in the future?" You will see something that, to some degree, you can do differently. Through this practice, you increase the clarity of your **<u>A</u>wareness**, empowering you to function more effectively.

"T" Stands For <u>T</u>ime

The stress you cause yourself by rushing makes it more difficult for you to deal with everything in life, including your child's behavior. When in the midst of rush, you might presume that you have a child-discipline problem when, in fact, you really have a time-management problem.

Routinely rushing makes maintaining your self-control impossible. The more you rush, the less patience you have and the more you overreact with anger and stress. Your lack of patience may make it seem as if your child intentionally does things to annoy you, like moving more slowly than usual, when in fact he may be doing the best he can. With more patience and more time, you will find that your child moves at a perfect speed.

When you notice yourself rushing, either slow down or stop. Re-examine the facts of your situation and take a good look at what you really need to accomplish before taking further action. Rushing signals the need to stop and think more clearly about what really has to get done. As a general rule, the more you rush, the faster you go nowhere.

Whenever you enter a "hurry-up" mode, you have spent too much time on what did not have to be done, or you have given yourself too little time to do what needs to be done. The remedy for this is to take more time for planning and organizing. You can eliminate 95 percent of the rush from your life by taking complete responsibility for the pace at which you live your life. Others may make demands upon your time, but how you respond to those demands remains entirely up to you.

Rush clouds reason. If you believe you must rush, you believe this only because your rush has caused you to think unclearly. *The decision to rush through life is always a hasty one.* Fear and error are the holes in which we land after jumping to hasty conclusions. Enough time always exists to do patiently, pleasantly and skillfully whatever you need to accomplish. If you constantly feel pressed for time, look for where you waste time or where you unnecessarily impose false deadlines upon yourself that require you to bear another torturous "time-crunch."

Admittedly, we live in a "hurry-up" society. Yet, this may not bode well for the fate of our wonderful world. Billions of people rushing generates maelstroms of chaos, causing countless accidents, misjudgments and costly mistakes. How many of the world's problems would be solved or avoided if we were not in so much of a hurry to finish things?

The next time you find yourself feeling angry and frustrated, instead of barking at the children try simply slowing down and dropping the "hurry-up" mode for 30 seconds. Thirty seconds of easing the pressure upon yourself can be enough to restore your peace and poise and allow you to function at a higher level.

The masters of time management all agree that to make the best use of your time you must regularly stop to clearly review your true priorities. For a sane life, you must give yourself time for planning, for considering options, for mentally clarifying your real needs and true goals. One well-thought-out action rewards more than 10 thousand hasty, impulsive actions. To state it in the simplest terms, rush makes it harder to parent in love; therefore, give yourself enough **Time** to move patiently through the experiences of your life, especially the experiences you share with your child.

"E' Stands For Energy

You cannot routinely violate your **Energy** limitations without serious consequences. A low energy level makes you more susceptible to illness and accidents, as well as to unbalanced, destructive emotional reactions. A low energy state also lowers your level of functioning in all areas and turns the normal and natural challenges of parenting into increasingly difficult and unpleasant burdens. When you feel tired or low in energy, you have less power to control or influence your circumstances. Then, it might seem like your child has a behavior problem when actually the problem you experience stems from your struggle to control more than you can.

You always possess more than enough energy to do what needs to be done while still enjoying the present moment. You do not have to come home from work too exhausted to patiently do the best you can with and for your child. If you seem to lack the energy you need, do not blame the demands your life or your child apparently place upon you. Your energy level depends entirely upon your own energy management.

If you find yourself becoming irritable with your child, consider the possibility that you may have allowed your energy level to fall too low. When feelings of stress or irritability arise, stop struggling to control your child, desist from all criticizing and complaining and start resting yourself. Rest gives your energy the chance to replenish. Rest by ceasing or diminishing your thinking, speaking and action and by becoming emotionally neutral.

The instant you begin to feel low in energy, immediately start doing less, thinking less, speaking less. If you continue to push past your point of tiredness you wear out the "instrument" of your body and mind, thus impairing how you function. When you feel your energy decreasing, discipline yourself to react as little as possible, to ease up and to lighten up. Do what you must in as slow and relaxed a manner as possible, and take *nothing* seriously.

Through The G.A.T.E.

As you practice self-control, your self-control *grows* (G) by degrees. As you practice *awareness* (A), you automatically gain the ability to adjust your actions and reactions for better results. As you create more *time* (T) by eliminating rush from your daily life and creating more *energy* (E) by respecting your energy limitations throughout the day, parenting with love becomes possible.

◆

◆

PART II

INFLUENCES THAT SHAPE YOUR CHILD'S BEHAVIOR

◆

6

The Art Of Pleasing And Displeasing Your Child

While on a long car trip, eight-year-old Ellen asked her mother to stop at a particular fast-food restaurant for lunch. Her mother explained that the particular restaurant Ellen had requested was not located at this exit of the highway, and there was no telling how long they would have to drive before they reached one. Ellen plunged into one of her typical sulking routines.

Although Ellen's sulking soon strained her mother's nerves, her mother realized that the only thing she could do that would not worsen the situation was to silently and patiently maintain her own emotional balance. Children may use sulking, in part at least, to make their parents react. By offering no reaction, Ellen's mother taught her daughter that manipulative sulking did not work.

Kindness, Not Weakness

Excessively harsh child discipline backfires. Kindness and compassion toward your child -- even when disciplining -- elicit kindness and compassion from your child. Do not confuse kindness with weakness, however. Being in charge requires the strength to endure your child's displeasure. If you permit your child's whining, sulking or tantrums to control you, your child learns to use those negative behaviors for control. If you make hasty efforts to rescue your child from her own negative feelings, she will have more difficulty learning how to deal with her feelings in a healthy, responsible way.

Balance

To practice effective child discipline parents must perform a true balancing act. Being too harsh and inflexible causes children more unhappiness and frustration than necessary, thus inciting angry, overly-aggressive or domineering behavior. Overly-permissive parenting confuses children about appropriate boundaries, responsibility and respect, which gives them the need to constantly test their parents' reactions to their behaviors in an effort to find limits.

Communication Boundaries

Let's look at an example of how this principle works. Throughout the day, Alec behaved shockingly. He exhibited rudeness toward his mother and toward other adults. He shoved other children out of his way. He ignored his mother when she told him to stop doing cartwheels so close to his baby sister. Then, as usual, he played with his video game while waiting for dinner.

Alec received no consequences for his irresponsible behavior. His mother pleaded, nagged and argued with him all day, but for all her talk she took no action to make his appropriate boundaries clear. Instead, he was allowed the privilege of playing with his video game. When asked why she did not take this away as a consequence for his behavior, she gave two reasons. First, she knew how much he liked playing with his video game, and she wanted him to be happy. Second, if she imposed that consequence, Alec would have thrown a tantrum and what she wanted was peace.

Nothing may be more humiliating or damaging to your child's self-esteem than feeling overly dominated by his parent, with the exception, perhaps, of being raised by a parent who appears indifferent. When you do not make your child accountable for his actions, he does not learn that his actions really count.

Your Child Needs To Feel Some Control

Respect your child's need to feel some degree of control over his own life by giving him choices instead of directions whenever possible and by using a positive, loving attitude when you direct him. Inspire, encourage, entice your child to do what you want him to do. *Lovingly* persuade him. Try to work *with* instead of against his feelings and his will.

However, do not confuse these positive means of guiding his behavior with begging, nagging or bribing your child. Begging and nagging portray you as a victim and teaches your child to disrespect and to dominate you. Bribing your child confuses his values and teaches him to do the right thing for the wrong reason.

Actions Speak Louder Than Words

When her mother was on the telephone, four-year-old Melissa screamed and cried solely to get her mother's attention. Melissa's mother finally turned to her and said, "If you continue to behave in this way, there will be a consequence."

Melissa shouted back, "No!"

Her mother shouted back, "Oh, yes, there will be."

Melissa actually started to smile as she shouted back, "No, there won't be!"

Her mother argued back, "I'm your mother, and I say there will be!" This argument continued and escalated until Melissa's mother had to hang up the phone to deal with her child.

Arguing with Melissa was pointless and unnecessary. Wasting your effort and energy in this manner weakens you and causes you stress, which, in turn, makes it more difficult to effectively guide your child's behavior. Melissa's mother did not have to convince Melissa beforehand that a consequence would follow her poor behavior, she merely had to follow through and prove that what she said was true.

Preparations For The "Real World"

Do not make the common mistake of presuming that your anger, impatience and criticalness prepare your child for the harsh realities of the world. The opposite proves to be true. Unnecessarily hurting your child's feelings weakens, rather than strengthens, her emotional stability. The child who receives an abundance of love and respect receives the best preparation for functioning well under the sometimes cruel and brutal pressures of this world.

However, a child who has grown accustomed to being overly indulged may appear deeply hurt and angry when parents begin to establish better limits. Only you, in the moment, can recognize whether your child's pain expresses a legitimate need or a false one. By maintaining your peace and poise in the face of his reaction, and observing patiently, your judgment has the best chance of being most accurate.

◆

7

Parenting With Integrity

Your behavior powerfully influences the way your child behaves, for children naturally and automatically adopt the behavior patterns of the people around them. Do you overstep your bounds, act and react recklessly, demonstrate a lack of consideration for others or a lack of respect for yourself, or behave in an overly self-centered manner? Such behavior patterns become imprinted upon your child's formation process, which then recreates similar patterns in your child's personality. However, by striving to express your higher potential you positively influence your child's behavior, strength of character and personality development.

Integrity And Consequences

Since your child receives much of his behavioral education from the way you behave, your misalignment with your sense of integrity in any area of your life brings out disturbing behavior in your child. Thus, dishonesty reaps dishonesty, aggression begets aggression and so forth.

When you live counter to your true sense of integrity, you become angry at yourself for not behaving in the manner you know is right. Just as a parent might feel a child should be punished for "wrong" behavior, you subconsciously believe and, therefore, transmit the "signal" that you deserve to be punished for being out of integrity. Other people in your life subconsciously respond to this signal and accommodate you. Thus, you draw to yourself people and circumstances that treat you harshly. As a parent who feels this way, you naturally draw out your child's potential to mistreat you as well.

The Roots Of A Child's Behavior

A parent recently called me to discuss her child's "behavior problem." Her seven-year-old son was treating her with defiance and disrespect, even going so far as to physically shove her and then challenge her to hit him. She informed me that her husband had used spanking to discipline him, and there had been times when the child's body showed bruises from the physical punishment he had received.

It seemed obvious to me that the father's hitting contributed to the child's physical aggression, but I probed further to look for insight into the mother's role in his behavior. I asked her to tell me about herself. She said she was separated from her husband and in the process of divorce. After further discussion, she admitted that currently she was in a relationship with another man, an affair she had begun before she left her husband.

I asked her how she felt about her conduct in this extramarital affair. Instead of answering my question, she explained that her husband was insensitive and emotionally unavailable. I asked her again to tell me how she felt about *her own* behavior. It took a while, but she finally told me she felt guilty about her extramarital affair.

Then, I pointed out how her indiscretion and the guilty feelings it naturally aroused could affect her child's behavior. The defiance, anger and lack of respect the boy was demonstrating toward his mother may have been a manifestation of the way she subconsciously felt she deserved to be treated.

Her sobbing began. Deep down inside, she said, she had sensed this might be the case. She admitted that she felt her conduct had lacked integrity and that she wished she had exercised more self-restraint by waiting for the proper time to begin a new relationship.

At that point she made a personal commitment to exercise more honorable self-control. This new attitude, combined with more self-honesty, made her feel better about herself and instantly empowered her to set more firm and appropriate boundaries for the child. This resulted in clear and definite improvements in the way her child related with her. During one of our subsequent talks, she said, "We admonish children to honor their parents, but we make it hard for them to do this when the parents dishonor themselves."

If your child's behavior has been causing you problems, take a closer look at the problems you cause yourself and others through your own actions and reactions. In what ways are *you* out of control? In what areas of your life do *you* go too far, or not far enough? Where do *your* character weaknesses lie? Answer honestly, and then work on improving or changing those aspects of your character to bring out the best in your child.

An Integral Element

Integrity involves taking responsibility for our affects upon others. It involves making the interests of others equal to our own. It means viewing the needs of others in a way that makes them consistent, rather than inconsistent, with our own needs. It is and integral element for parenting with love.

♦

8

The Law Of Reflection

Even parents who feel completely out of control of their children's behavior exert a powerful influence on that behavior. Your child's behavior, mood, attitude, and values reflect back the behavior, moods, attitudes, and values expressed in her environment, and you, as her parent, most definitely play a central role in that reflection process.

This reflection of environmental influences, called "The Law of Reflection," largely governs your child's behavior. As Maria Montessori, the great visionary of child development, taught, we must consider the environment first when looking for the cause of a child's behavior problems.

The Foundation Plane

The psychological states, which means the thoughts, feelings, attitudes, and values, conveyed through the people and conditions surrounding your child shape your child's personality, as do the more visible behavior patterns of speech and action. The younger the child, the more deep and lasting the impact of his environmental influences. During the first six years of life, for instance, your child's basic character and underlying personality traits take shape as the foundation plane of his development. Thus, the environmental factors present during that time play a huge role in shaping his personality, and these traits are ones with which he then must contend in his adulthood.

You Radiate What You Are

Your thoughts, feelings, attitudes, and values emanate. You literally radiate your conscious and unconscious personality patterns, which your child then absorbs and adopts in her own unique way. Therefore, to truly understand your child's behavior, you must first understand yourself.

As a child, I perpetually felt impatient. I could not stand waiting for what I wanted. My father bitterly complained about and criticized me for this, but he never dreamed of looking more closely at himself to see how he contributed to these patterns. He overlooked the connection, for example, between his impatience when my mother failed to have dinner ready on time, and my impatience with waiting for what I wanted. My impatience directly reflected his own.

Using the Law of Reflection to better understand your child's behavior does not mean that you should blame yourself for that behavior. Rather, it serves to empower you with a new understanding of how to work with your child. In my case, my father could have assisted me in developing the patience he wanted me to possess by practicing more patience himself, especially while we shared time together.

Observe The Law At Work

To prove the power of The Law of Reflection, try this experiment. Observe your child's behavior closely for a few days, and notice which behavior patterns and personality traits you find most disturbing or difficult. Then, spend a few days closely observing your own behavior to see when, where and how you demonstrate those same behaviors and personal qualities.

To utilize the Law of Reflection, begin consciously and intentionally practicing the kinds of behaviors you want from your child. You might practice being more considerate, patient, respectful of others and yourself, more self-disciplined, more responsible, more courteous, kind, calm, and loving.

A Child's Aggression

One mother recently told me this story: "This morning my five-year-old son pushed his three-year-old sister very hard, causing her head to hit the wall. She cried a lot. I sent him to a time out, but it didn't seem to bother him. In fact, on the way to his room he grinned at me. Soon after his time-out ended, he locked his sister out of the house. All I could think of doing was to give him another time out, but I knew it would work no better than the first time."

Applying the Law of Reflection to this situation, the mother could have looked at her son's behavior as a reflection of some aspect of her personality. The boy's anger and physical aggression may have reflected her own feelings of anger and aggression, which she consciously or unconsciously expresses. This does not mean that she necessarily behaves *exactly* as the boy does. However, if she were to improve her handling of her own emotional intensity, she *automatically* would provide her child with a more loving, peaceful influence. And, in turn, his behavior would begin reflecting those qualities.

The Consequences You Administer

Using the Law of Reflection does not necessarily exclude the use of consequences aimed at encouraging your child's self-discipline. However, *only* giving your child negative consequences for misbehavior may accomplish nothing. Your anger and aggressiveness continue to influence your child, even though you might administer the harshest consequences when your child demonstrates these patterns himself.

In fact, the very consequences you use may reinforce the behavior you oppose. For instance, if the consequence you impose includes losing your temper and screaming at your child, you impress that same way of reacting upon your child's malleable personality. Shouting at a child for shouting at you makes about as much sense as arguing with your own echo. You cannot provide your child with better self-control by losing yours.

Strive To Function At Your Highest Level

As you better manage *yourself*, your child automatically becomes more manageable, because he receives the influence of your wise functioning. Work on your reactions to your child's actions. Do not focus so much on your child's behavior that you overlook your own behavior. If you lose your temper when your child's play continues after you have asked him to stop or when his play becomes too wild, your angry, impatient reaction teaches him to lose his self-control when things do not go his way.

The more intelligently you respond to your child's behavior, the more intelligent the behavior patterns you pass on to your child. To find more intelligent responses, begin focusing on your own thoughts, feelings, speech, and actions, as well as noticing the results they achieve. Begin gradually eliminating the useless stress and strain you cause yourself and others by the way you react to events and situations. Bring more awareness, wisdom, peace, order, love, and joy into your strategies and responses, and strive to function at your highest level in all things. As a result, your child's behavior will improve automatically, because it will become a reflection of your own growth.

Self-Discovery

The Law of Reflection explains why taking a good, honest look at yourself just might be the most helpful and important thing you can do for your child. As you face your own personality patterns, you can make constructive adjustments in your own behavior, and, in the process, avoid passing problematic patterns on to your child.

Applying The Law of Reflection makes parenting easier. Instead of futilely fighting against your child's irritating behavior patterns, which you yourself unwittingly help create, demonstrate more of the higher level of functioning you want from your child. As your child reflects your own improved behavior, you have less of a need to discipline her behavior.

Using the Law of Reflection is quite easy. For instance, if your child demonstrates insecurity, take a close look at your own feelings of insecurity. Virtually every so-called "strong-willed child" has at least one stubborn parent who insists on dominating the child and perpetuating power-struggles. Ask yourself, "Am I this parent?" You also can think about issues this way: If your child often expresses anger, for example, she is communicating through her behavior that you or your spouse (or both of you) need to work on the anger you feel within yourselves.

As mentioned earlier, using The Law of Reflection does not necessarily override the need for other disciplinary measures. For example, you may discourage your child's whining by not giving the child attention for this behavior. You empower that to which you give your attention. If you let a child's whining control you, the child learns to whine to get her way. However, we need to look deeper. Whining expresses helplessness and dependency. By examining yourself closely and rooting out your own tendencies to express these weak character traits, you may do much toward eliminating your child's whining.

Self-Work

Stated in the simplest terms, using the Law of Reflection means working on *yourself* to positively affect your child's behavior. Improving your behavior can improve your child's level of compliance and respect, transform such difficult daily routines as bedtime and mealtime into smooth routines and raise your child's self-esteem and positive motivation.

No Separation

Even when separated from one another by space and time, your behavior affects your child's behavior. Divorced parents living away from their children continue having a kind of psychic link with their children. So, if you feel anger toward your x-spouse, you may unwittingly contribute to your child's abusive behavior toward that parent. If you experience hostility, anger, depression, or insecurity in general, even though your child dwells in another town, her mood, attitude and behavior may be influenced by your states of mind and heart.

What You Bring Home

The way you act and react from moment to moment, whether you are with your child or not, shape your personality patterns and, therefore, affect your child's development. Every time you become angry or critical at work, for example, you strengthen and deepen that behavior pattern in your personality. When you come home, you bring home with you all of the angry and critical personality patterns you are fed during the day. Remember that both your inner and outer behavior patterns radiate from you and impress themselves upon your child's forming personality. Thus, the way you behave outside the home returns home with you and your behavior then transfers these characteristics to your child. If you exhibit domineering, manipulative, insensitive, or ruthless behavior at the office, be prepared to return home to a little tyrant.

Responding Purposefully

A parent observed his child angrily strike another child with a plastic bat. The typical parental response to this kind of behavior includes an aggressive, angry reaction directed toward the child, but does this child really need anger directed at him? Of course not.

To use the Law of Reflection in such a situation, you first need to clarify your objectives. What do you want to achieve? Obviously, you want your child to exercise stronger self-control and to treat others with kindness and without angry, physical aggression. Knowing this, the way to achieve it becomes clear. You can state firmly and clearly, but without anger or even a raised voice, that hitting other children is not allowed. A firm response demonstrates the strength of self-control you want your child to exhibit.

Then, you need to shift gears and exhibit kindness by placing the incident behind your child and yourself. By treating your child with both firm strength and loving kindness, you reinforce those qualities in your child's personality.

Finally, you need to be careful not to impulsively strike your child in response to his violent act. By not resorting to violence yourself, you reinforce your child's capacity to choose more humane and less destructive ways of responding to difficulty.

Before you respond to your child's behavior, think about the kind of behavior you want your child to demonstrate. Then, demonstrate that behavior. In other words, give your child the behavior you want in return.

♦

9

Your Child's S.T.E.M. Universe

Since your child's behavior patterns reflect the patterns of influence she receives from her environment, you support your child's potential to behave well by creating environments for her that reflect the kind of behavior you want her to exhibit. In other words, by creating an environment of order, beauty, peace, love, and harmony, you make it easier for your child to behave in orderly, beautiful, peaceful, loving, and harmonious ways.

Your Child's S.T.E.M. Universe

Your child's environment includes the **Space-Time-Energy-Matter** coordinates of his experience, which Isidore Friedman referred to as his "S.T.E.M. Universe." These include the general pattern of your child's surroundings (space), his daily schedule or routine (time), the physical and psychological forces that impact upon him (energy), and the qualities and conditions of the material objects around him (matter).

As you take charge of these four essential factors influencing your child's behavior, you contribute to your child's orderly, harmonious self-expression. Thus, by bringing order and harmony into your child's S.T.E.M. Universe, you avoid contributing to your child's problematic tendencies and take full advantage of your opportunity to bring out your child's best.

Creating order, harmony, love, and peace in your child's S.T.E.M. Universe helps him behave in happy, loving, orderly, and intelligent ways. Any chaos, discord, conflict, or anger in your child's S.T.E.M. Universe contributes to his angry, combative, chaotic drives and tendencies.

Your Universe

Carefully observe your feelings to see how *your* S.T.E.M. Universe affects *you*. You know that when you walk slowly through a place of beauty and peace your entire being feels uplifted.   However, surround yourself with an environment containing disorder, dirt and angry, rushing people, and then try functioning in that inharmonious space. You will find yourself more prone toward rushing, behaving in a disorganized fashion and generally feeling and functioning more negatively.

If you become selective about the environment you provide for yourself, you can provide yourself with more peaceful, harmonizing, loving influences.   Doing this for yourself can make you a better parent, because the better you feel, the better you will behave and respond and the better will be your child-management skills.

Just as you feel more soothed, calmed and harmonized by carefully selected environmental influences, your child's state changes according to the environmental influences he receives. Since you want your child to be more calm and settled to the extent possible, avoid exposing him to loud, wild, hectic, intense environments.

A child's S.T.E.M. Universe affects his feelings and behavior more profoundly than yours, because children are more sensitive and open to environmental stimuli.   The S.T.E.M. Universe influences children most deeply and enduringly during the first six years of life.   So, providing carefully selected environmental influences is most important during these years.

The Positive Power Of A Loving Environment

I recently heard the following story: A woman gave birth prematurely to twin boys. The size of the boys differed drastically, so the doctors placed them in separate incubators. The doctors did not expect the smaller of the two boys to survive, and, as expected, the vital life signs of the smaller one began fading immediately.

The mother of the boys looked on in desperation as the plight of her child worsened by the minute. Just as it became evident that the smaller infant had arrived at death's threshold, the mother picked him up and placed him in the same incubator with his brother. The larger boy instantly placed his arms around his smaller, dying brother, and continued holding him in that loving embrace. Soon the smaller child's vital signs began to show slow but steady signs of improvement. In a short time, the crisis had passed, and both children survived.

This story demonstrates the change that can occur by changing a child's surroundings to ensure it includes as much love and warmth and acceptance as possible. Every hug and kiss and every loving word and gentle touch you give your child provides him with a loving environmental influence.

How To Take Charge Of Your Child's Universe

Every day, look for simple, easy ways to improve your child's S.T.E.M. Universe. To begin, bring more order, harmony, beauty, peace, and love into her surroundings. Create your child's environment to match the kind of behavior, feelings, moods, and attitudes you want her to demonstrate. Expose her to pleasant and interesting, orderly and calming sights, sounds, smells, and textures. Eliminate or replace broken or damaged objects. Let each corner of every room be as neat, organized, in good repair, and clean as possible. Fill her living space with plenty of light and fresh air.

Create soothing, harmonious atmospheres for your child through soft lighting, muted colors, gentle sounds, and the presence of flowers. These small, simple changes in your child's environment will have an observable effect upon her attitude and behavior.

The Function Of Time

Just as your child needs order in his surrounding physical environment, he also needs order and regularity in time. An orderly schedule and regular daily routine provide your child with the temporal support he needs to behave in happy, orderly ways. An orderly schedule makes your child feel secure and helps him develop self-discipline.

Children behave and perform better when they know exactly what to expect. Unpredictability in your child's daily routine may make him more prone to anger, inflexibility, boredom, restlessness, jumpiness, nervousness, unhappiness, and insecurity. If your child's daily routine demonstrates chaos, so will his behavior. To change this, bring more regularity and order into his daily schedule and routine.

Helping Both You And Your Child

Bringing regularity into your child's daily life helps both you and your child. You will find this especially true if you have more than one child. The more well-planned and regular your children's routine, the easier it becomes for you to keep things functioning smoothly. A stable routine helps you get into a flowing rhythm that everyone soon follows with little effort.

Create stable, set routines for morning departure, nap, lunch, play, dinner, and bed times. If your child's behavior continues to be a problem, consider experimenting with changes in her routine, and when you find a routine that works, stick to it.

Establish family traditions, such as dining as a family every night, having special Saturday morning breakfasts or

Sunday early dinners and set holiday routines. If you live without a stable structure upon which everyone can rely, your family's unity will prove more stressful and difficult to maintain.

When you and your child know what to expect from day to day, your child will feel more comfortable and you can better plan and strategize your own activities around the stable structure you have created. Living impetuously and without plans increases the stress of parenting and makes life harder on your child. In such a situation you will find yourself blaming your frustration with your child's behavior on your child, when the problem has more to do with the fact that he needs a more structured daily routine.

Problem-Creating Environments

Exposing a child to a great deal of rush, blaring background television noise, angry arguments, and mess makes it more difficult for your child to behave with the tranquillity and order you want her to express. Hyperactive children especially need to have their exposure to stressful situations, rush and commotion minimized as much as possible.

Observe the general surroundings inundating our children today. Is it any wonder that children exhibit so many problems? Children walk outside into roaring, rushing traffic with frustrated adults screaming at one another in impatient, unforgiving anger. An enormous amount of chaos, stress and conflict surround children every day.

Re-Examine Your Child's S.T.E.M. Universe

Routinely re-examine your child's S.T.E.M. factors and evaluate their influence upon you child. You do not have to be some kind of expert to do this skillfully. Just look at the influences and imagine how you would feel and act if exposed to them every day. If you do not like how they make you feel or behave, change them to better accommodate harmonious feelings and behaviors in yourself. Your child's feelings and behaviors will follow suit.

Even small changes and adjustments in the environment can produce better results in your child's behavior *and in your own*. It does not take more money to create more orderly, harmonious, peaceful environments. Make whatever changes you can with the resources you have at your disposal. Look for mess, clutter, broken objects, faded colors, dust, or grime, and improve those conditions to some degree. Every little bit helps.

Your Place In Your Child's Universe

Always remember that you represent your child's key environmental influence. Your state of being and the way you function greatly impact your child's behavior. Therefore, especially when you are with your child, keep your emotions tranquil and loving, your mind clear and centered, your awareness focused on your present experience or activity. This provides your child with a calming, centering influence.

When your child repeatedly gets into mischief, siblings pick on one another or three children demand different things from you all at the same time, discipline *yourself* to be among the influences in your child's environment that support peace and harmony. Stay committed to *being* your child's best influence by enjoying your parenting experience with peace, poise, patience, and love.

If your behavior often includes being intense, rushed, or nervous, start making small improvements in your daily mode of being. Relax a little more. Slow down even slightly. Begin functioning *somewhat* more calmly. This helps your child become more calm, relaxed and orderly.

The Role Of The Parents' Relationship

The way parents relate with one another also comprises a central role in a child's S.T.E.M. Universe and, therefore, deeply affects his behavior. Your responsibilities to your child include your development of the skills and self-control you need to relate in a wise, compassionate and dignifies way with your child's other parent, and this is true whether you are married, separated or divorced.

Develop your ability to relate with your child's other parent in a respectful manner, even if you feel the other person is being disrespectful, without losing respect for yourself.

You cannot control your child's other parent, but you can express your best in the relationship. While your child's behavior reflects the behavior demonstrated by both parents, as well as by the over-all tenor of the relationship between those parents, at best you can but dedicate yourself to the expression of your own highest potential. As long as you do your best, you provide your child with at least one positive influence in his life.

S.T.E.M. Parenting

Ordering your child's S.T.E.M. Universe serves as an indirect way of supporting your child's behavior. This easy and effective aspect of parenting provides your child with more of the calming, ordering influences she needs to give you the happy, orderly behavior you want for her.

The more nurturing and supportive the influences your child receives from you and the environment you provide, the more constructive his behavior will be even when he finds himself in unsupportive surroundings which you cannot control.

◆

10

The S.E.A.T. Of Your Authority

Having true authority in your relationship with your child means not needing to use force or intimidation to gain control. It means your child does what you ask because he *wants* to do it. He wants to please you, to assist you, to live up to your belief in him and his belief in himself.

Three essential elements help you achieve true, positive authority in relationship with your child:

1. Belief in yourself,
2. Belief in your child, and
3. Authority over yourself.

Belief in yourself means you possess confidence in your competence and in your essential worth as a human being. Belief in your child means you refuse to see the child as anything less than worthwhile and highly capable. Authority over yourself means you intelligently rule your actions and reactions instead of being ruled by automatic, unthinking action and reaction habits.

The S.E.A.T. Of Authority

A simple formula, called "The S.E.A.T. of Authority," can help you aim for positive, loving authority in your relationship with your child. The S.E.A.T. of Authority highlights four basic elements -- **S**peech, **E**motion, **A**ction, and **T**hought -- that influence your dealings with your child. By applying The S.E.A.T. of Authority to the elements mentioned above -- belief in yourself, belief in your child, and authority over yourself -- you can guide your child with less anger or stress.

"S" is for Speech

Building Belief In Yourself: Express and develop your self-confidence by speaking with a voice of authority. Listen to the sound of your voice, and instill in it the attitude of belief in yourself. Listen to the way you speak about yourself, and be careful to talk about yourself in a respectful manner but without boasting. Speak as if you expect your choices and decisions work.

Building Belief In Your Child: Speak respectfully to your child. Talk to her as if she truly is a worthwhile human being. Do not refer to her as a brat or a wild animal. Avoid insensitive criticism and put-downs of any kind. Do not talk to her as if she is helpless, pathetic, evil or inferior in any way. Monitor what you say so your words empower and inspire her belief in herself rather than her self-doubt and so she recognizes your sincere recognition and acceptance. As you speak to her, be aware of how she emotionally responds to your statements.

Building Authority Over Yourself: As a daily exercise, practice being in more conscious, intelligent, loving control of your power of speech. If your child argues that you are not fair, you do not have to argue back. If you enter into a draining, stressful argument, you have lost control over your speech. Be on the alert to notice and eliminate your own useless, negative and destructive speech habits of criticism, complaining, pleading, arguing, nagging, and screaming.

As you practice using speech more consciously and effectively, your growing authority over your speech will result in your growing authority in your relationship with your child.

"E" is for Emotion

Building Belief In Yourself: Notice how you feel about yourself. Having true humility does not require you to regard yourself as inadequate, worthless or inferior. You must believe in yourself *emotionally* to experience peace and power. Deepen your *feeling* of yourself as worthwhile. The way you feel about yourself influences the way you express yourself. Confidence precedes competence. As you practice intentionally *feeling* good about yourself and acknowledging your worth in your feelings, you naturally express your higher potential. Since others reflect the way we feel about ourselves, your self-respect inspires your child's respect for you.

Building Belief In Your Child: Your belief in your child also needs an emotional base. In other words, you have to *feel* your belief in your child. Build up your emotional belief in your child by thinking about her with love. The more deeply emotional your belief in your child, the more healthy and strong his self-esteem will be. Think of your child as if you thoroughly believe in him. He will fell this attitude coming from you and be inspired.

Building Authority Over Yourself: Establish intelligent authority over your emotional reactions, moods and attitudes. Discipline yourself to believe with deep emotional conviction that the things you truly want to happen in life are destined to happen. Discipline yourself to maintain this positive attitude even during the toughest times. When it feels natural to feel sad or angry, let those feelings flow, but do not let them run you. If you observe them patiently and without tension, they naturally will return to inner peace. You earn your child's trust and respect as he sees that he can count on your emotional stability. His confidence in you grows as he sees that his mistakes do not trigger an automatic blow-up from you, and that your love, acceptance and approval are constant.

"A" is for Action

Building Belief In Yourself: Act boldly. Be willing to play. Try new challenges. Do things new ways. Express confidence in your physical movements by standing tall and walking as if you possess total confidence in yourself and in your life, yet do this without bravado. Practice doing all things in a smooth, easy, pleasant manner that expresses inner joy and peace. Make a list of your greatest goals and highest dreams, and begin taking some kind of action toward them. As you move toward your heart's desire, you motivate your children to move with you. Perhaps your goal is to have better control over your eating habits. Take action in line with your highest visions and your children cannot help but look up to you.

Building Belief In Your Child: Take actions that convey to your child your trust and confidence in her. Treat her body as sacred, her feelings as important, her thoughts and ideas as valid and meaningful. Avoid doing too much for her, for that conveys your belief in her helplessness. Give her opportunities to do things for herself, to lead, to make her own decisions, and to learn from the consequences. Give her freedom. Give her space. Treating your child as competent, responsible and trustworthy brings out her potential to demonstrate those qualities. Demonstrating your trust in her through action inspires her trusting willingness to actively cooperate with you.

Building Authority Over Yourself: Be self-directed in your actions. Do not automatically do what others ask or demand. First, consider if doing what they want adequately respects your time, energy or other resources. Notice when you allow others to control you because your timidity holds you back from asserting yourself. Notice when you feel like you are giving too much, giving to the point that it is really not doing anyone any good. Then, resolve to take more control over your actions. As you establish more wise and self-respectful control over your actions, your child learns to place higher value on what you do for him and on what he can do for you.

"T" is for Thought

Building Belief In Yourself: Thoughts really provide the foundation of authority, because your thoughts determine your speech, emotions and actions. Thinking is equivalent to speaking inside yourself. What you think radiates outward, thus affecting your behavior as well as the thoughts and behavior of those around you. Tell yourself mentally, over and over again, that you believe in yourself. Think thoughts that affirm, "I am valuable and worthwhile" and drop thoughts that regard you as less. Ultimately, you become whatever you imagine yourself to be. Tell yourself over and over that you are in charge, that you practice perfect parenting, that your children love and respect you. The reality you conceive within yourself is the reality to which you give birth in your outer life.

Building Belief In Your Child: You decide in what manner you think about your child. Since your child always deserves your respect and acceptance, you can choose to focus on that. This decision depends upon you and your authority over your own mind. Whatever you think about, you support. The more you think about what your child does well and right, the more you will see him doing right and the more you will support that behavior with your thoughts. The more you think about what he does poorly and wrong, the more wrong you will see.

Before permitting a thought about your child to hold your attention, ask yourself: "Am I focusing on a quality I want to empower?" If not, focus on a quality you do want to empower. Your constructive thoughts about your child strengthen his respect for himself and for you.

Building Authority Over Yourself: Just as with your speech, emotional reactions and physical activities, you need to control your thoughts. Your whole life follows the direction of your thought. What you think about you create, attract and empower. What you concentrate your thoughts upon expands into your experiences. Use your thoughts efficiently, and make the most of the great power of thought. As you gain conscious, intelligent control over your thinking, your power of authority literally makes you the competent, confident "head" of your relationship with your child.

◆

11

Your Child's Self-Creation

To a significant degree, the quality of your child's behavior depends upon the way you handle his normal, natural behavior, feelings, limitations, abilities, and needs.

In this chapter, we will focus on what children under the age of six need from their parents to behave well. If your child is older, the information here may help you better understand some of the problems you now face with your child. This, in turn, can help you make adjustments in the way you relate with your child for better outcomes.

The Foundation

The foundation of your child's personality and character development forms during the first six years of life. During this period, your child requires an abundance of:

- **loving feelings**
- **non-critical attention**
- **respect**
- **appreciation**
- **approval**
- **affection**
- **freedom of activity (freedom to do as he chooses)**

- **freedom to explore his environment**
- **freedom to express his feelings**
- **clear and consistently-upheld boundaries that keep his energy involved in constructive activity and out of destructive activity**

Sensitivity To Order

Children under the age of six have a deep sensitivity to order. This means that to feel happy and to behave as harmoniously as possible they need to be placed in orderly environments. They also require order in their daily schedule or routine.

In addition to this, children between the ages of two and six exhibit a strong need to order and to arrange the objects and people that surround them. Provide them with the opportunity to satisfy this need. However, be careful to not go too far or you may allow your child to overly dominate you; this would establish overly domineering behavior patterns.

Mastery

Between the ages of two and six, a child's natural sensitivity for order translates into a desire for mastery. This makes these years the ideal time for teaching your child the basic rules of grace and courtesy as well as of appropriate and responsible behavior.

Simply defined, "grace and courtesy" mean an orderly, careful way of doing things as well as displaying good manners, which includes table manners, sharing and being courteous to other children and adults. By appropriate behavior, I mean socially acceptable forms and safe ways of behaving. For instance, a child needs to learn not to pound on glass doors, walk on furniture, scream without reason, or spit in public places. Responsible behavior means cleaning up after oneself, dressing and undressing oneself, caring for one's own room and belongings, contributing to the household by completing chores.

From the age of two to six children are most open to instruction in these areas, because doing things according to clear and consistent guidelines or rules satisfies their craving for a sense of accomplishment, mastery, order, and control.

Learning

Children under the age of six learn through observation and practice. Demonstrate what you want your child to do, and give her the opportunity to practice or repeat the activity as often as she likes.

Children under six do not require lengthy, complicated explanations as to why things are to be done a certain way. Make simple statements, such as "We do not pound on glass doors, because glass can break," or "You are not permitted to run around the restaurant, because it disturbs other people," or "We ask someone to 'please let us pass' instead of pushing them out of the way, because it makes them feel better."

If a demonstration of how you want your child to behave along with a simple explanation as to why you want her to behave that way does not work, remain patient and non-critical. Do not strain yourself to continue explaining or arguing. Your child simply may be testing you. Or, he may need more demonstration and practice to establish the pattern. (For additional actions you can take to encourage desired behavior, refer to Part III of this book.)

The Sacred Ceremony Of Self-Creation

Children grow, learn and develop at a deeper level and to a greater extent during the first six years of their lives than in all of the following years combined. Virtually every personality pattern and character asset and deficit we face as adults can be traced back to our experiences during these early years.

As a child fingers a simple object, such as the grating of a shopping cart, or practices the execution of a simple task, such as pushing the cart, she advances her physical and psychological development. She gains understanding of how things work and of how she works. She exercises her concentration, her senses and her dexterity.

If we were to truly grasp the vast significance of each moment of the young child's experience, we would observe the child with awe and reverence, for each moment of the child's day represents *a sacred ceremony of self-creation.*

The Importance Of Completion And Repetition

Children under the age of six need and want to complete what they start, and they need and want to repeat what they do. Completion gives them a sense of order. Repetition increases their mastery, thus providing them with increased self-esteem. Permitting your child to complete and to repeat activities and tasks not only develops the abilities required to accomplish the task, it also builds the general skills of concentration, completion and persistence.

Therefore, whenever possible, avoid needlessly interrupting your child's completion or repetition of an activity. Not only will the interruption irritate and annoy your child, but if you interrupt your child's natural cycle of activity too frequently he misses the opportunity to develop his basic concentration, perseverance and self-discipline skills during these most deeply formative years.

Surprise!

A parent's surprising entrance into a child's environment when order has been established *without* the parent creates confusion for the child. Such a break disturbs a young child's equanimity and sets off problematic behavior. For instance, many preschool teachers, nannies and other caregivers have observed that children behave well *until their mothers show up*. The instant a child becomes aware of her mother's arrival, she starts acting out in disturbing ways.

The parent's arrival interrupts and disrupts the order established for the child. Children under six generally require as much preparation as possible for transition, and, subsequently, an easing into that transition. By suddenly discovering the arrival of her mother at her preschool, a child becomes unclear about who has authority in the situation. In this case, not only the unpredictability of the situation but also its ambiguity contribute to the child's misbehavior. The child's excitement about seeing her mother, and her intense desire for the mother's attention, further contribute to her self-indulgent behavior.

It would be best for you to avoid such a sudden intrusion and to prepare your child for the interruption when it is going to be necessary. You can prepare your child by talking about it beforehand and by having the caregiver frequently remind your child of what to expect and of how he is expected to behave when it happens. Also, by understanding what is happening with your child, both parent and caregiver can remain calmer in the face of your child's antics. This makes it easier for your child to settle down than would your nervous, tense, confused reactions.

The Most Suitable Environment

If your child frequently finds inappropriate objects to handle or with which to play, adjust the environment so that you do not constantly need to direct or correct the child. As you just read, interfering with your child's natural activity cycles disrespects a child's basic need and that can worsen her behavior. Remove or gate-off those objects you do not want your child to handle rather than constantly taking objects away from her or using force or aggression to police her.

Children learn correct behavior by watching the behavior of those around them. If you constantly take things out of your child's hands, thus upsetting the child, the child learns to aggressively seize what he wants without concern for how others feel about it. If you use much force or aggression to make the child do as you say, the child learns to be forceful, pushy and overly aggressive in his relationship with you and others.

We mistakenly presume that we can teach discipline and compliance to children younger than six by giving them orders and fiercely insisting they obey. In many instances, however, the child does not have the control over himself necessary to comply -- even if he had the desire to comply. Also, the more anger and aggression you express toward or around the child, the more angry and aggressive the child becomes. This, in turn, produces more defiance, not compliance.

By providing your young child with environments in which intervention in her activities is kept to the barest minimum, your child naturally develops the self-reliance and self-esteem she needs to behave appropriately and responsibly later. These characteristics will serve you and your child well when you have to trust her in less controlled environments.

As a general rule, the more the environment permits your child to do things for himself without your assistance and the more it keeps him out of trouble without parental interference, the more suitable the environment. The more suitable the environment, the more easily your child develops the happy, appropriate behavior patterns you want him to exhibit.

♦

12

The Building Of Your Child's Personality

Your child's personality develops, or "constructs," as he passes through four basic developmental planes:

> **Plane 1: birth to six years**
> **Plane 2: six to 12 years**
> **Plane 3: 12 to 18 years**
> **Plane 4: 18 to 24 years**

Planes of development are like tiers of a structure, one built upon the other. As the child advances from plane to plane, the others remain with him, holding up the complete structure.

Past Influence

The key to understanding behavior patterns that appear in the latter planes requires knowing how earlier planes were constructed. For example, if you had a critical parent, especially during the first six years of your life, since that time you probably have suffered painful feelings of low self-esteem. In addition, you probably have gravitated toward critical people who judge you in negative ways, because their treatment of you corresponds with your sense of who you are and what you deserve. Your critical parent did not mean for you to feel and behave this way; however, criticizing a young child often produces this long-term result.

Understanding And Change

Understanding how your early childhood experiences contributed to the formation of your personality helps you overcome the limits these experiences imposed on your development. When you see, for instance, that your lack of self-esteem is not an intrinsic part of you but a result of your natural childhood response to treatment you received, you can change your response in the present and begin relating with yourself and with others as someone truly worthwhile. Your self-esteem then improves, as does your treatment of others.

Understanding how your behavior affects your child's development helps you adjust your reactions to his behavior so your responses produce the positive outcomes you want.

No Criticism

One constant for each plane of development proves to be the negative impact of angry criticism. Criticizing your child to the point of shaming him makes it harder for him fulfill his true potential. When you criticize your child, you run the risk of lowering his self-image and convincing him that he somehow is not the way he should be. This actually reinforces the behavior pattern that bothers you.

As you grow in the understanding of each developmental plane, you will see positive ways to bring out desirable behavior in your child.

By meeting the unique needs and taking advantage of the unique opportunities present during each developmental plane, you provide your child with the kind of support that helps her to be her happiest, to fulfill her highest potential and to behave her best. In the sections that follow, we will examine some of the essential influences impacting a child's behavior in each specific plane.

Parenting For Plane 1

During the first plane of your child's development, from birth to six years, he experiences the peak of his natural sensitivity to order and his readiness to develop careful patterns of behavior. Take advantage of this fact. Since children in the first plane learn primarily through observation, patiently demonstrate placing things back in their rightful place, cleaning up after yourself and exhibiting general neatness. Take the time to show, rather than to merely tell, your child exactly what you want him to do and how you want him to do it. This includes showing him how to replace the cap on the toothpaste and how to put his clean laundry away. Children in this plane also learn through active engagement. Patiently involve the child in ordering, organizing and neatening activities.

As you read in the previous chapter, virtually every personality strength and weakness you experience on a daily basis is rooted in your experiences during the first plane of life. The reason for this lies in the fact that, during this time, almost every influence to which a child is exposed penetrates to the deepest levels of her psyche. A young child's consciousness has few, if any, barriers to taking in information and experience; the mind functions like a totally absorbent sponge. Therefore, make every effort to provide your child with the highest and best influences possible. Read to her from Shakespeare. Play Mozart in the background. Hang beautiful art upon the walls. Take her to beautiful, quiet natural spaces. Behave with the utmost grace and composure around her. Exposure to chaos, commotion, conflict, harshness, cruelty, or discord will not emotionally strengthen your child; these influences emotionally weaken your child instead.

The behavior patterns and general influences your child receives while passing through this plane become deeply embedded in her personality structure. If, while in this plane, your child receives or witnesses much anger, criticism or impatience, she will reflect these in her later behavior and adopt them as lasting patterns at deep levels. If she is exposed to love, peace, poise, and support, she will adopt these as lasting patterns and exhibit them in her later behavior.

Never Too Late

If your child is older, do not despair. It is never too late to change. As you alter your approach to parenting, you impact your child at a core level because parents possess a deep connection to the very essence of how the child feels about himself and how he functions.

Constructive Activity

Any activity upon which your child concentrates represents a constructive one, and constructive activities range from piling sticks gathered in the back yard to putting toys away, from placing objects in a row in the order of their sizes or color to touching every other key on the piano. Merely examining an object that holds interest for your child constitutes a constructive activity.

As your child engages in constructive activity, he becomes peaceful and happy, develops greater self-discipline, strengthens his ability to concentrate, and learns from the experience. For example, as your infant examines your car keys, placing them in his mouth and manipulating them with his fingers, he learns about taste, develops self-control, improves his dexterity, and gains knowledge and understanding of the universe. Even the infant's intellectual abilities develop as he manipulates his fingers.

Select activities in which your child wants to engage. Needlessly forcing a child to do something increases her will to defy you and other authority figures.

Anchoring The Senses

During the first plane of his life, anchor your child's physical senses to the physical world. Keeping your child's attention alertly focused on the details and relationships of the physical universe balances her emotions, prepares her for practical life, sharpens her alertness, develops her intellect, and strengthens her self-control. It also develops her control over her imagination, thus making her less prone to imaginary fears of the dark or of sleeping alone.

Keep your child's eyes, ears, nose, taste, and touch engaged in conscious, focused exploration or examination of the physical universe. When he becomes bored, give him something upon which to focus his eyes, something to smell, to taste, to hear, to feel. Act as if you find the sensation very interesting.

Invite your child to listen to the sound of one object and then the sound of another object so she can hear the relationship between the two sounds. You do not need elaborate equipment for this. Without speaking, tap on a tissue box and point to your ear as you listen. Then, hold a tissue and tap on that, listening to the almost inaudible sound that makes. Go back and forth from one sound to the other to communicate to your child non-verbally the difference between the two sounds.

Anchoring To Order

Every child needs an opportunity to freely express his natural urge for wild, unstructured activity. In fact, giving your child a time and place to run around and scream like a wild person helps him settle down and behave in a more orderly manner afterwards.

Your child also requires activities that help him center himself and concentrate his forces in an organized way. To accomplish this, involve your child's mind and activities in patterns of order instead of chaos. This practice, called "Anchoring to Order," grounds his behavior to order, so your child will easily and naturally behave in an orderly fashion.

Give your child the opportunity to create physical order. Let him arrange pots or cups in an ordered sequence according to sizes or let him do this with his blocks. As the child creates order he builds his power to behave in orderly ways. He also prepares his mind for orderly, intelligent thinking in his next developmental plane.

In this first plane, your child's sensitivity to order requires him to have neat and orderly environments and an orderly, regular schedule as well. When it comes to bringing out your child's orderly, cooperative behavior, surrounding him with order proves to be as important as engaging the child in orderly activity.

Anchoring To Real, Practical Life

Children in the first plane of development instinctively want to do what they see being done. They prefer helping you with chores to swinging on a swing set. They prefer washing a window to playing with a dollhouse. We adults just assume that fantasy play makes children happier than more practical work, because our parents believed this about us.

Anchoring your child's activities to real, practical life means allowing and encouraging her to participate in activities that meaningfully contribute to the household, and which prepare her for more advanced practical work. This brings the child real joy.

Allow your two-year-old child to handle a real hammer, not just a plastic, make-believe hammer. Allow your three-year-old child to help you mow the lawn, not merely trot beside you with his bubble-blowing, plastic, make-believe mower. Involving your child in the practical work of real chores, not just make-believe ones, connects his mental and physical habits to the world of practical life. Doing so at an early age pays off later, when he naturally will exhibit more motivation, interest, confidence, and competence in responsible, practical work.

Self-Reliance And Independence

Throughout each stage of your child's development, make one of your principal, guiding aims the preparation of your child for independent self-reliance. Support your child's power to help himself. Teach him how to do for himself the things you normally do for him, and give him the chance to practice them.

From the age of two, carry your child minimally. This encourages him to walk on his own two feet in this, and in every other, area of life. Encourage self-reliance in a kind and loving way. The child of three already can dress herself, care for her room, make breakfast or lunch for herself (if you prepare the environment so she can reach what she needs easily), and even show her two-year-old sibling how to do the things that she does. Just show her how to do what you want done, and give her practice.

Giving your child more responsibility for himself makes him happier and develops his healthy self-confidence. At the same time, your child's self-reliance serves you, because the more he can do for himself, the less energy you have to spend doing those things for him.

Place your child in prepared environments where you can allow him plenty of freedom. The child who has a sufficient amount of freedom will be more accepting of the necessary restraints and restrictions you must impose.

Influence Through Demonstration

Influence your child's first plane behavior the most easily by consistently demonstrating the behavior you want. Both your internal behavior (thoughts, feelings, moods, values, and attitudes) and external behavior (speech and actions) influence your child's behavior and development. Children raised in a house where the parents argue with one another develop an arguing pattern. Children raised in a home where one parent speaks to or treats the other parent cruelly develop a cruelty pattern. Children raised around an angry, irritable adult who needs to feel in control at all times develop an angry, controlling pattern in themselves.

To help your child develop better self-control and more respect for others, demonstrate those patterns around your child. To assist your child's development of more industrious behavior, be more industrious around your child. To help your child break his addiction to watching television, resist your urge to watch. To help your child be more relaxed and less domineering, practice maintaining your peace and poise around her and eliminating any excessive, unnecessary efforts to control her. Even the youngest infant registers and receives the subtlest influences.

◆

13

Parenting Keys For
The Second-Plane Child

As your child moves into her second plane of development a major metamorphosis from infancy into childhood takes place, and you must change with your child. You have to let go of your "baby" and relate with your child as an independent, responsible individual.

You allow your child to feel and act more grown up and responsible by *treating* her as if you expect her to be that way. Parents often complain that their seven-year-olds have reverted to three-year-old behavior. One possible cause may be that the parents are still relating with the child as if she was irresponsible, incapable and in need of constantly being directed and corrected. Give your child more freedom to do things her own way and in her own time, and you may find more mature behavior blossoming from her in response.

Of course, your child still needs boundaries clearly and consistently established. However, you now can give your child more opportunity to show you what he can do on his own before assuming he needs you to supervise or assist.

Your Child's Way Might Work

Give your child problems to solve. If he has not been doing his chores in a timely manner, have a talk (not an argument) about it. Tell him when you want the chores done, and put his chore schedule in writing. Ask him how he feels about the schedule. Be open to his suggestions and be willing to make reasonable compromises. If he wants to do the chores on a different time table or in a different order, do not panic.

Consider the issue. More ways of doing something adequately always exist. If you have a problem with his suggestions, tell him the problem and invite him to suggest possible solutions.

Lack of Preparation

If your child was not well prepared for order in the previous plane of development, do not expect her suddenly to become Ms. Neatness now. You may have to be rather firm about her picking up after herself. However, if you establish the rules clearly and consistently and follow the general guidelines of child discipline you are reading in this book, you can raise her level of performance in this area.

Do Not Argue

As your child passes his sixth year, his reasoning and verbal abilities mature, and one of the toughest challenges becomes the ease with which you fall into an argument with him. If this happens to you, you may suddenly find yourself wondering why you became so excited over his first words during infancy!

When you give a direction, state it clearly and *state it only once or twice.* Do not endlessly repeat yourself, automatically raise your voice or allow yourself to react with much frustration if your child complains about your direction. Do not waste one ounce of your energy on a single unnecessary word. If you can reasonably assume that he understood what you told him, either listen to what your child has to say without emotion or walk away.

Your Arguing Habit

You can save yourself a tremendous amount of otherwise-wasted energy by disciplining yourself to break *your* habit of arguing with your child. The instant you catch yourself arguing with her, just *STOP*. Instead of arguing, silently think about what you want to accomplish with your child, and then take action in line with the outcome you want to achieve. End arguments that simply.

Make An Appointment

While arguing proves destructive, constructive discussions remain necessary. The difference between a destructive argument and a constructive conversation lies in the fact that during an argument no one really listens.

Let your child know you are open to discuss any problems *at the appropriate time.* Explain that, from now on, when he wants to discuss a problem with you he can make an appointment. The next time he argues or complains spontaneously, say to him, "I can see that you have some problem with this. Do you want to make an appointment?" If the present moment seems like a good time for a discussion, you can choose that time to talk. If it does not, he has to settle for a time that works for you.

Sympathetic Agreement

During constructive conversations, it generally works best to give your child a chance to express his complaint or argument for a short while at the beginning of your discussion. If his argument makes sense, you may change your mind about the issue under discussion. If your mind has not been changed, you might say something like, "What you said made sense. I know how hard it can be to do something that you really don't want to do, but I have to insist here."

Showing genuine concern for your child's feelings instantly creates something called "Sympathetic Agreement." Sympathetic Agreement turns an emotional conflict into a base of mutual accord. You can build upon agreement but not upon conflict. Eliminate the ego factor from your response to your child's complaints or criticism. Accept the fact that he does not have to want to do what you say nor does he have to agree with your opinions. Accept the fact that he needs to know you truly care about how he feels for him to truly care about himself and others.

Emergence Of The "Abstract Mind"

In the second plane, your child's "Abstract Mind" emerges. Abstract Mind refers to his ability to think about things he only can imagine. He now has the power to ponder more deeply the consequences and ramifications of his actions, and at this time you can reach your child and influence his behavior by discussing things with him in greater depth.

In this plane, to behave in orderly ways your child needs an orderly mind. So, help him understand how things work. Do not just give the child facts. Weave the facts into interesting concepts. If you do not have answers to his questions, conduct some research. As your child gains a clearer, factual understanding of the universe, his ability to think and to behave rationally develops.

Anchoring The Abstract Mind

In the first plane of development, you anchored the child to the physical world and to practical life through his physical senses and activities. In the second plane, anchor the child through his mind. At this stage, your child needs her imagination harnessed to factual reality. In other words, she benefits more by contemplating and exploring the realities that interest her than mere fantasies. This does not mean that fantasy must be totally shunned but that factuality must be stressed.

Take advantage of your child's new ability to understand cosmic facts. Appeal to her fascination with the gigantic size of mountains, the microscopic life on her finger tips, bizarre natural phenomena, surprising customs, and distant places. Point her mind to the stars!

Feeding your child's hunger for learning about facts she finds fascinating keeps her interest and motivation tethered to reality, honesty and accuracy. This makes it easier for her to recognize her responsibilities to other people, to herself, to other living creatures, and to her environment. The child in the second plane seeks orientation to the cosmos and will demonstrate better adjustment as her sense of her place in the universe evolves.

Teaching

Guide the mental activity of your second-plane child just as you guided her physical activity in the previous plane: with kind firmness, patience and love.

If your six-to-12-year-old seems unmotivated to learn, look at the teacher to find a possible solution. The teacher carries responsibility for motivating the student to learn. If the teacher cannot handle that responsibility, find a tutor capable of igniting your child's natural passion for learning.

Adapt the mode of teaching to your child's abilities to concentrate, rate of learning, sensitivities, and interests. Any subject can be presented in a way that captivates the student's ardent curiosity; the teacher who doubts this should not teach.

Bonding

The child who feels a deep, positive bond with his parents feels good about himself and behaves in more respectful, responsible ways. In the first plane of development, bonding occurs by providing the child with abundant love, attention, affection and sensitive responsiveness. Just being with your child in the first plane of builds your bond.

Bonding with children between the ages of six and twelve can be achieved by giving them your trust in and respect for their abilities, feelings, thoughts and independent self-reliance. Also, bonding is created by having long, deep discussions about whatever interests the children and by joining the children on learning adventures. Even through natural, scientific or cultural pursuits that interest you both, like expeditions to the library, zoo, park, or museum with your child can foster a bond.

Time For Moral Education

In the second plane of development, your child has the capacity to learn about morals. His mind now permits him to handle abstract concepts, such as honesty, friendship, loyalty, forgiveness, and responsibility. These concepts represent ideas and are, therefore, known as "abstract" because you cannot point to them in the physical world. Prior to this plane, abstract concepts held little or no meaning for your child. Simple words, such as "nice," or explanations, such as "it makes a person feel better when you say 'please' in front of a request," sufficed. Now, you can actually help your child live up to these abstract concepts through discussion.

The "Herd Instinct"

The second-plane child experiences a kind of "herd instinct" that draws her toward groups outside the family. She learns from group activities and thrives on belonging to a group of friends, a team or a club. This represents a natural progression in your child's social maturation process.

During the first three years of life, your child requires little more than his immediate family and home to satisfy his need for social involvement and environmental experience. From the age of three to six, she exhibits a readiness to spend a few hours a day away from home and Mama in a home-like preschool.

In the second plane, your child's mind thrives on exploration of the whole universe while, at the same time, personally he gravitates toward social groups, teams and clubs. His group, or "herd," experiences make *real* his practical understanding of the importance of teamwork, his significant impact on others and his responsibility toward them.

◆

14

Parenting Teens

Your child enters a the third plane of development at around age 12, and this plane lasts through about her eighteenth year of life. Plane 3 brings about changes in your child that affect her so profoundly both physically and psychologically that this period can be regarded almost as a new birth.

Your Influence

Since you now have about 80 percent less influence upon your child's development than you had during his first six years of life, do not waste your effort trying to mold his basic personality in major ways. For example, you no longer can "create" a more responsible, respectful, orderly person. His head is full of his own ideas of right and wrong and he is determined to live out those ideas.

However, there still remains much that you can do to influence his behavior. While you can no longer teach him right from wrong, you probably will have to establish the boundaries for right and wrong that you will accept. He does not have to agree with your values, but if he expects to have your support and cooperation he needs to live by your rules.

The "Terrible Teens"

Remember those "terrible two" years? They usually occur when your child turns about two-and-a-half, that difficult age when nothing seemed to make your child happy and she became very vocal about telling or showing you so. During that period, she probably demonstrated angry frustration for no apparent reason. Recall those years and then observe your teen. You may find some striking similarity in the attitudes of the child then and now.

Your toddler expressed so much unhappiness because she lacked the ability to do the things she saw being done around her. She felt restrained by her natural limitations and by the control of other people. She could not understand that this frustrating phase was just temporary. The early teen years place your child in a similar situation, thus, your teenager may feel and behave in a similar fashion.

Your teen child sees adults around him making the rules and doing as they choose, but he cannot make his own rules nor live entirely in his own way. Authority figures treat him as if he knows nothing, and he knows just enough to think that he understands everything but not enough to realize how much he has to learn. Your teen's world lacks congruence, and he feels normal frustration about this fact.

A good deal of your teen's negativity and rebelliousness comes as naturally as physical growing pains felt by young children. So, try not to take your teen's disturbing attitudes personally. How she feels may have nothing to do with you, and her feelings largely may be out of your control. Just as you had to endure some of her moody defiance and sudden tantrums in her toddler years, you now have to create your own peace and patience as your child suffers through another one of life's unavoidable trials.

You Can Help

You can help your child by accepting what she is experiencing. Keep in mind the fact that her hurtful words and angry actions express the way she really feels about herself. Your teen's inescapable frustrations make her moody, anxious, nervous, irritable, hypersensitive, insecure, and perhaps even explosive. Teens often feel their emotional pain just does not make sense. By understanding her discomfort, and showing that you sympathize, your love acts like a spiritual cushion, making your teen's pain a little more bearable.

Letting Go

You may help your teen most by getting out of the way; carefully avoid over-involving yourself in his affairs. Encourage his responsible behavior by demonstrating trust. Be firm when necessary but only when letting your child choose for himself proves not to work. Do not struggle to solve her problems - be there to listen and support her in her efforts to solve theses issues for herself in her own way.

Teens still need to know that certain rules must be followed, and from time to time you will need to back up your rules with consequences (restriction of privileges). However, do not make the serious error of treating your adolescent as a child, or your condescending attitude or excessive involvement may trigger rebellious behavior.

Bonding With Your Teen

Your teen has a deep yearning for practical life wisdom, and this fact offers you the opportunity for positive bonding. You may be surprised to learn how much valuable life wisdom you possess, and how much your teen appreciates receiving it from you once you begin sharing your insights without condescension or judgment.

In the first plane of development, you bonded with your child by providing an abundance of loving attention and physical presence. In the second plane, you had the opportunity to bond with your child intellectually through rational discussions about subjects of interest to your child. Now, in the third plane, you have the opportunity to bond with your child in her pursuit of practical life wisdom and understanding.

Engage in discussions about life, death, love, sex, money, career, religion and any other deep or personal issues in which your child shows interest. Do not try forcing your teen to accept your point of view. Strive, first, to understand your teen's questions. Then, share your insights to the degree that the teen is open to receiving them.

As you connect with your teen as her counselor, she will view the relationship as truly sacred and will demonstrate a higher, deeper kind of respect and appreciation for you than she previously was able.

The Quest For Identity

In the first plane of development, your child identifies himself with whomever or whatever surrounds him. He picks up traits from parents and siblings as well as from pets. In the second plane, your child's quest for identity reaches out to friends and social groups, such as sporting teams and scout groups. In the third plane, your teen seeks an identity through role models or "teen idols." The teen strives to emulate those she most respects and admires.

The Problem With Teen Idols

Your child's teen idol may not present worthwhile role models. In fact, music, television or movie stars may present totally inappropriate models due to the immoral values and illegal or abusive behavior and lifestyles they sometime exhibit.

By demonstrating sincere respect and appreciation for your teens' values, sensitivities, interests, and *genuine* needs you can help your teen find appropriate role models or move yourself into the position of a role model in her life.

Be patient and understanding with your teen's experimentation with different looks and changing mannerisms. If you impose too much control, she feels babied, which may ignite her desire for even more outrageous behavior. Together, you and your teen might go on a quest looking for a way of dressing, applying make-up or wearing her hair that you both find acceptable. Together, you might also look for role models that personify traits and values you both can appreciate.

Anchoring

Teens need anchoring in the real world and hunger for real life experience that traditional classroom environments do not provide. The teen who gravitates toward a dangerous crowd might make different choices in friends if his parents help, encourage or allow him to work at a job that introduces him to earthy, hard-working, tough-minded adults. Such a job gives him the sense of confidence he needs while, at the same time, providing him with practical experience that helps him work at loftier positions later in life. If you are overly protective or overly possessive with your teen it hurts his self-esteem and may prompt self-destructive behavior.

Teens And Friends

You must accept that throughout your child's life a steady movement away from you occurs. By the time your child reaches the middle teen years, friends become more important than family. She will probably want to spend more time away from you than with you. Resist the temptation to take any of this personally.

You help your teen make the "right" choices by trusting her and showing her respect. However, limits still need to be established. Inform your teen that she earns the privilege of being with her friends, driving, and doing other activities that you allow by fulfilling her responsibilities *first*. These include school performance and her contribution to the household through chores and general cooperation. The price she pays for not fulfilling her responsibilities is a loss of the privileges she enjoys. As long as you relate with your teen in a respectful, adult manner, your establishment of reasonable rules will be acceptable to her. However, she may work very hard to argue them away.

Parenting In The Fourth Plane

In regard to parenting, by the time you child reaches the age of 18, in regards to parenting, less equals more. Your young adult wants to work out his problems on his own. Lend a supportive attitude and a listening ear, but do not be surprised if you get chastised for offering unasked for advise. The young adult needs to define his own point of view.

At this stage of life, the young adult finds inspiration in ideals. She may still need some help in her pursuit of her dream, and in the fulfillment of her sense of her life-mission. Support in a way that helps her do her best, avoiding perpetuating her dependency on you.

Just as your involvement must recede, so must your support. The 18 or 19 year old who comes and goes as he pleases, treats his parents and siblings disrespectfully or rejects the rules of common decency in the home is ready to be on his own. If you coddle the young adult out of your own fear of what he will do to himself, you ensure that his irresponsible patterns will continue and lodge even more deeply.

◆

15

Lose The Critic

Take a look at this mathematical formula of child behavior:

$$\infty P - C = SI = B$$

The symbols represent: Infinite (∞) Potential (P) minus (-) Criticism (C) equals (=) Self Image (SI) equals (=) Behavior (B).

Now look at the first part of this equation, ∞P. All human beings possess infinite potential. Your child has infinite potential, and so do you. "Then why does my child's behavior seem less than perfect?" you might ask. Maybe because he has received -- and accepted as true -- negative criticism about himself. Receiving a lot of criticism lowers our self-image, which, in turn, lowers our level of behavior.

False Assumption Of The Past

In the past, we believed we could help a child behave more appropriately and perform at a higher level by fiercely criticizing his mistakes and shortcomings. However, now we know that children who receive much harsh criticism tend to suffer from low self-esteem and low self-confidence, which hampers their competence. Also, these children are more likely to develop harsh, angry, critical habits of their own.

Negative criticism makes it harder for human beings to excel. Think back to the last time someone harshly criticized you. How much more motivated were you to change? How did you feel about yourself? How did you feel about the person criticizing you? Did you receive much criticism in your early childhood? If you did, you can probably recall periods when you experienced a lack of confidence and a poor self-image. These represent direct and natural responses to negative criticism.

Dealing With Criticism

Children erect emotional walls in response to criticism. This explains why using "put-downs" to discipline children of any age makes it harder to reach and teach them. When criticized in a manner that wounds the child emotionally, your child feels misunderstood, unappreciated and resentful, which diminishes her desire and motivation to try to do better. Without the motivation or desire to learn a better way, your child does not want to hear what you have to say. Also, because your criticism is painful, she feels hurt and angry and unwilling to be close to you.

As adults, we have some power to detach from the derogatory treatment and criticism other's direct our way and to regard it as just their opinions and not as a reflection of our true selves. Even as adults, however, accomplishing this point of view can take real effort. Whether we reach this perspective or not, in just about any relationship the more harsh and angry criticism we direct at the other person or that is directed at us the more the relationship deteriorates.

Children, especially in the first six years of life, have virtually no defense to protect themselves from the critical attitudes projected upon them. As your child enters the second plane of development (age six to 12), you can begin explaining to him how to deal with criticism. You can tell your child that the opinions we hold of ourselves are the only opinions that either can lift us up or bring us down. You can explain that by giving ourselves positive messages about ourselves, thinking of ourselves in ways that build our confidence and belief in ourselves as well as our self-respect, we can overcome a good deal of the negative, critical messages we may have received from others or will receive in the future.

Criticism Creates

Making a big deal about your child's misconduct may encourage her to do worse instead of better. Think of your words as the building blocks of your child's self-image. By labeling your child "rude", "bossy", "wild", "obnoxious", "lazy", "selfish", or "bad", your words create that image of herself in her mind. Her subsequent behavior then automatically follows the pattern of that image.

Constructive Criticism

You can constructively criticize, but this takes much sensitivity and self-control. In particular, you need a great awareness of your intent. If anger or the desire to hurt your child's feelings motivate your criticism, your child receives a negative, rather than a positive message.

Be aware of your child's response to your words. See and sense your child's feelings and attitudes as you pay attention to your child's subtle reactions to your words. If your child responds by shutting down, erecting defensive walls or becoming angry, stop focusing on his mistake. Let the matter go, at least for now. Reconsider the message you want to convey and the results you want it to achieve. Then, try again later, with a more loving, accepting attitude.

Lose The Critic

When you feel the urge to attack your child, pay close attention. If you look closely, you will see within you the face and feel the feelings of your own most-critical parent. The early criticism you received from your parents taught you to treat -- or to mistreat – those who disappoint you as inadequate and inferior. When you feel like indulging in angry criticism toward yourself or your child, remind yourself that you, like the critical parent before you, pass this pattern on to your child by allowing it to rule you, by allowing yourself to express it toward your child.

The more criticism you received in childhood, the more prone to criticizing you are likely to be. When you work on ending your negative, destructive criticalness, you may be shocked at the difficulty of this endeavor. Forgive yourself many mistakes. Each time you slip, acknowledge to yourself that you slipped, and then start your practice over again (you can apologize to your child as well). Forgiving yourself will make you less prone to criticizing and more prone to understanding your child.

◆

◆

<u>PART III</u>

DISCIPLINE WITH LOVE OPTIONS

◆

16

Your Power Of Positive Visioning

One of the parenting powers you possess lies in your ability to determine what mental image of your child you hold. Your *positive vision* of your child behaving well, for example, empowers you and your child to achieve that behavior.

Let us say, for instance, that lately you have felt frustrated by your child's excessive crying. Spend time every day picturing in your mind the way you would prefer your child to feel and to behave. See her happy, content and smiling. See yourself relaxed and comfortable around her. This makes achieving the changes you envision easier.

The best educators have long known about and successfully applied the power of "Positive Visioning," the technique used in the example above. These teachers consistently envision their students focused on their work and interacting harmoniously with their teachers and with each other. Parents of more than one child should find this information especially helpful since the larger your group the more necessary planning, forethought and preparation becomes.

Apply Positive Visioning To Child Discipline

Positive Visioning entails constructing a vision -- a clear, positive picture or image in your mind -- of a condition you want to create. In the child discipline process, your vision would consist of a positive picture of your parenting skills, your child's behavior and your relationship with your child.

Try this exercise: Think of your child's most bothersome behavior. For instance, you might feel annoyed when he does not pick up after himself. Next, think of the way you react to this behavior. Remember your frustration, your stress or any other emotional reaction you experienced when you last saw your child behaving in that disturbing way. Also recall what you may have said or done as a reaction. Did you scream? Did you argue? Did you hit? Did you feel humiliated? Did you try to intimidate him with angry threats?

Seeing what you want to change provides the springboard for seeing the way you want things to be. So, now imagine the way you prefer your child to behave. In that vision, also see the way you want to feel and act around your child. For instance, see your child picking up after himself without being told. See yourself calm, confident and happy with your child.

Re-empower this positive vision through repetition. Each time you re-focus on the positive vision of your child behaving well and re-experience the positive feelings you associate with that vision, you feed the process of making it happen.   If you then look for signs of progress and opportunities for further advancement, you will find them.

A Positive Visioning Exercise

Positive Visioning does not always work this dramatically. However, it does always lead to new ways of making at least small improvements that create real life scenes more closely matching your positive visions. The image upon which you consistently focus functions like a blueprint of what your actions ultimately create.

Make a list of the kinds of behaviors you want from your child. Review that list and imagine your child behaving in that manner and the positive feelings you associate with him doing so. For instance, see your teen and yourself having calm, loving discussions instead of heated arguments, and allow yourself to experience the good feelings that would bring you.

Do this for each change you want. Each time you exercise your power to positively envision a change, you free yourself from the worry and strengthen your ability to envision and achieve the results you want with your child.

Envisioning Yourself

Positive Visioning gives you a way to improve your responses to your child. Many parents feel disappointed in themselves when they hear themselves yelling at their children after swearing they would never do so again. Take charge of your reactions by regularly envisioning yourself parenting with more peace, poise and power. Imagine yourself feeling relaxed, in charge and confident. Picture yourself patiently guiding and successfully directing your child with confidence and love. See the relationship you want between you and your child -- the two of you getting along, loving, respecting, and cooperating with each other.

See Solutions

Positive Visioning provides a key for creating solutions to problems. For instance, you may not know how you can provide your child with everything she needs to be as happy and well behaved as possible, but you can begin to imagine your child in that perfect situation. Focusing on this vision gives your creativity a direction. Your mind starts working and soon comes up with possible options for bringing reality closer to your vision.

See your child's life in a way that provides her with the best support. Imagine an orderly daily routine. Imagine her having all the time she needs with you. Imagine yourself as the happy, patient, strong parent she needs you to be. See your children getting along. Create a vision of your financial success and career satisfaction providing you with the monetary and emotional means to provide your child with the physical necessities and positive attitude she needs from you.

The more you practice Positive Visioning the easier it becomes and the more your life changes to take on your envisioned characteristics. These changes may not occur instantly or all at once, however. In the beginning, you may simply find yourself being more aware of and recognizing opportunities that you ordinarily would have overlooked to achieve better results with your child. However, if you pay close attention to what happens in each moment, you will see immediate change to some degree.

Teach Your Child Positive Visioning

You can include your child in the practice of Positive Visioning, and teach your child how to use Positive Visioning. Begin by inviting the child to join you. Have him sit, lie or stand with his eyes closed while focusing on some positive outcome together. For instance, you can both envision him spending the night in his own bed *without* being afraid. If he has been having conflicts with his brother, you can suggest that he visualize the two of them getting along, respecting one another's property, helping one another instead of competing with one another. If your child gets teased by other children in school, have him visualize himself with friends in class, being liked and liking others, and laughing together. If your child complains that he hates doing his homework, have him visualize actually loving his homework and getting an A, or at least a B, every time.

If your child resists this practice, you can practice for her. See her getting along well with her classmates, loving her homework, sleeping in her own room through the night without fear. Your positive visions of your child's behavior, performance, attitudes, and experience become self-fulfilling prophesies.

◆

17

Your Power Of Positive Expectation

The steady, daily discipline of expecting your child to behave well and trusting that your child can be happy, healthy and well-adjusted, builds your power of Positive Expectation. Practicing Positive Expectation builds the base of inner strength you need to parent with a positive attitude and to pass that positive attitude to your child.

What You Expect

Whatever you *expect* consistently and persistently eventually happens. You have to pass through periods of disappointment along the way, but if you continue to believe in the possibility of success you will continue taking the actions necessary to achieve your goal.

Your expectations, like your visions, carry the power of self-fulfilling prophesies. Use this power simply by consistently and persistently *expecting* your child to behave well.

Overcoming Disappointment

When our expectations are not met, we feel disappointed. We then lower our expectations, or have negative expectations, because we fear feeling disappointed again. The lower our expectations, we think, the less likely we are to be disappointed. The tragic irony of lowering our expectations lies in the fact that, by so doing, we guarantee our disappointment. By expecting less, or expecting something that we do not want, we create the feeling of disappointment right from the start.

Realistic Expectations

Having positive expectations about your child does not mean living in denial of the true facts about your child's personality, behavior, needs, and limitations. You still must pay careful attention to your interactions with your child and recognize what he truly needs from you in the moment. However, as long as you have negative or lowered expectations of your child or yourself, which is the same as lacking belief in your child or in yourself, your efforts to help your child will lack the necessary power.

When you have realistic, positive expectations of your child, you believe in the possibility of him fulfilling his unlimited potential within the parameters of his own unique patterns. For instance, expecting an autistic child to become an extrovert would be unrealistic, but trusting that he can be more open and that he can lead a more meaningful, emotionally-balanced life within his inner world can be both positive *and* realistic expectations.

Expectations Create

Times arise when every parent feels inadequate. Use these times to grow instead of to pointlessly condemn yourself. To reduce your stress and improve your results with your child, develop positive expectations regarding your parenting ability.

Your expectations, positive or negative, draw to you the conditions you regard as your future. Positive expectations regarding your child's ability to behave well and your ability to parent well empower you and your child to create that reality.

Alertly recognize your expectations and, then, drop negative ones and build up more positive ones. Every moment you spend expecting what you do not want makes it harder to create what you do want.

Positive Affirmations

You can empower yourself with Positive Expectation through the use of positive verbal affirmations. By filling your mind with positive verbal statements you leave less space for negative thinking. At the same time, your statements to yourself eventually impact the way you feel and, in turn, what you create in your life.

Make a list of the ways you want your child to behave. Then, turn that list into a set of positive, verbal affirmations you say repeatedly to build your positive expectations. Say them when you catch yourself dwelling in a negative expectation about your child. For example, think of your child behaving in a particular way, and then state silently or aloud to yourself, "My child can behave this way." You may want to be more specific and make a statement like, "My child treats his little sister kindly," "My child and I get along well," or "My child sleeps through the night without crying."

If your child says she is unhappy and that she hates her life, think of her being happy and expect her to feel that way as you tell yourself, "My child can be happy and love her life."

Do not just state your positive affirmation; try to feel it being true right now. The more you repeat an affirmation and call up the feeling you would have if the statement was true already, the more powerfully your positive attitude works.

Expect Specific Changes

Use Positive Expectation to make specific changes. Think of your child's most-disturbing behaviors, and use positive expectations for each. Read the following examples created by parents at my workshops:

Behavior I want to change	Affirmation for positive expectation
My child screams out, "No," when I tell her to do something.	My child does what I ask of her and behaves in a respectful, compliant manner.
My child whines when he wants his way.	My child accepts my decisions and asks for what he wants in his normal tone.
My children ignore me when I speak to them.	My children listen to me when I speak to them and respond to me respectfully.
My children bicker incessantly.	My children get along and communicate with each other in a kind, pleasant manner.
My two-year old hits me when I tell her, "No."	My child keeps her hands to herself when I can't allow her to have her way.

You do not have to get specific when using affirmations to strengthen your positive belief in your child. Just tell yourself over and over, "My child behaves wonderfully." Say it and try to feel it, over and over and over again.

By working with affirmations, you can lower your stress level, raise your enthusiasm and increase your ability to create the relationship you want with your child.

Expect Your Own Great Life

Much of the anger, stress and strain parents feel in their relationships with their children have little or nothing to do with how the children behave. The parents' reactions stem from the general pressures they feel in their lives.

Changing your worries into positive expectations frees you from much of this stress, and, therefore, indirectly makes your relationship with your child more pleasant, peaceful and positive. So, expect all you want from life to happen, and your child will benefit from the effects of that positive expectation.

To begin expecting your own great life right now, think of three things that you would love to have happen in your life. Think of or picture in your mind each one happening. Do this for just a moment. In association with each thought state, "This can and will happen," and experience the feeling that you are destined to get what you want.

Develop The Positive Expectation Habit

Develop the habit of expecting your child to behave well in all situations. Notice when you expect him to behave in disturbing or disappointing ways, and shift into expecting him to behave even better than you can imagine.

Use the power of Positive Expectation to bring out your own best behavior. Make a list of the ways you tend to relate with your child that you would like to change. This might include reactions such as anger, stress, impatience, losing your temper, criticizing, screaming, complaining, arguing, or hitting. It might include doing too much for your child or being controlled by your child's manipulation. When you have completed the list, think of yourself exhibiting the parenting skills and strengths you want instead. Imagine yourself handling your child's behavior with greater confidence, competence and peace. And, expect that to happen.

◆

18

Conscious Detachment

When your child wants your attention, he might use extreme behavior to get it. Your reaction to that behavior determines the lesson he learns in that situation. Therefore, you can begin using your attention and reaction to his behavior as a consequence aimed at guiding him toward better self-control.

Avoid Rewarding Misbehavior

When your child screams, complains or pouts in an effort to force you to pay attention to him and you give him that attention, you reward and encourage that particular behavior. Even when you turn to your child with anger and criticism, you make him the center of your attention. This gives him the result he wants, since now your attention revolves around him.

To avoid rewarding when your child misbehaves to get attention or a reaction from you, consciously and intentionally detach your reaction from your child's action. By using "Conscious Detachment," you basically ignore your child's behavior and do not let it control you. At the same time, you focus on maintaining your peace and poise. Your child learns that misbehaving for attention or control does not work.

An Easy Method That Works

While Conscious Detachment may not always be the appropriate response to your child's behavior, such as when she does something too dangerous or excessive, it often proves to be the easiest and most effective way of discouraging problematic behavior. By using this technique, you expend the least amount of energy to teach and to guide your child through consequences, the consequence in this case being your non-reaction to your child's behavior.

When you use Conscious Detachment, you help your child learn, for example, that you do not respond to whining, that nagging does not control you, that you do not lose your balance in reaction to angry words, that you cannot be manipulated by tantrums, and that sibling rivalry does not dominate you. Since these behaviors no longer control you, your child has reason to stop using them to accomplish that goal. If, rather than using Conscious Detachment, you respond in a more typical fashion and with anger, your reaction may give your child exactly what he wanted -- your attention or your pain. Children soon discover that if they can upset you with specific behaviors, they can feel in charge by using those behaviors.

Conscious Detachment Starts Within

Truly effective Conscious Detachment starts *within*. You have to work on not reacting internally to your child's misbehavior. This means maintaining your emotional tranquillity.

Concentrate on remaining emotionally neutral the instant you become aware of your stressful reaction to your child's behavior. Remain emotionally detached from any behavior you wish to discourage. Do not reward misbehavior by overreacting. Your neutral, calm attitude unempowers behavior aimed at forcing you to feel powerless.

Conscious Detachment Buys Time

Conscious Detachment does not necessarily mean you will not respond to your child's misbehavior. This approach means you elect not to deal directly with the issue now. By not reacting, you allow yourself to think about the problem and formulate a well-thought strategy.

Sometimes Doing Less Accomplishes More

Judge each situation separately to see if Conscious Detachment will work best. When your child cries for attention, calmly consider if her need is genuine before giving her the attention she demands. If her behavior seems manipulative or her needs excessive, remain non-reactive. Take your time responding. Give her responsibility for meeting her own needs.

Making a big issue out of a child's poor performance can promote more problems, while overlooking the mistake and cutting the child some slack might permit the best outcome. Using Conscious Detachment means overlooking something your child has done that normally would upset you and cause you to react negatively. That negative reaction might have spurred your child on to repeat the behavior or to demonstrate even worse behavior, while Conscious Detachment discharges her drive to do so.

Positive Attention

Do not confuse Conscious Detachment with a withdrawal of your love and positive attention. When you use Conscious Detachment, you do not diminish the value of the child; you diminish the power of his negative behavior. Children need consistent love and approval from their parents. Children refused these emotions behave worse rather than better.

Your positive attention reinforces the behavior you want. Positive attention means consistently relating with your child as a sacred, worthwhile being.

If you have gotten into the habit of criticizing and correcting your child, you may be unintentionally discouraging *desirable* behavior. You may be overlooking times when your child complies, does try to please you or makes the effort to show you respect and appreciation.

Your authentic, positive responses encourage your child to repeat the behavior you appreciate. When you exhibit too little interest in your child's positive efforts, your child's motivation to make positive efforts diminishes or turns into the desire to rebel.

Letting It Go

Not reacting to a problem or disturbance means letting it go *for now.* Giving the problem a chance to pass on its own, instead of reacting as if you must somehow take control of every situation, lets you peacefully receive the support of the child's natural growth process. Letting something go often lets it go away, while reacting to or giving attention to it can sometimes lock it into your child' behavior patterns.

Some children respond to a parent's frequent efforts to control them with worsened behavior. It almost seems they instinctively know that if they behave badly many times in rapid succession they can have all the power and control they want.

Every reaction to your child's behavior uses your energy. You can exert only so much control over your child at any one time. Changing your child's behavior through Conscious Detachment helps you avoid exhaustion. If you strain and drain yourself by trying to control too much, you lower your energy and, subsequently, your level of effectiveness. In addition, the stress you cause yourself results in poor judgment and overreactions.

When you overreact, you run the risk of producing a hyperactive child. Letting your child's behavior go for the sake of maintaining your own emotional balance may demonstrate responsible behavior on your part. The next time you notice yourself about to react to your child, pause and consider if Conscious Detachment might not be your better option in that moment.

◆

19

Building

In the previous chapter, you learned how to avoid paying too much attention to unwanted behavior. Now I would like to discuss how to give your child positive 'attention to achieve positive results, for children thrive on adult attention supplied to them properly.

First, keep the following fundamental, two-fold child-motivation principle in mind at all times:

1. Giving a child negative (angry, impatient, annoyed) attention for undesirable behavior often encourages him to display more negative behavior.
2. Giving a child positive attention (acceptance, approval, appreciation) encourages him to display more positive behavior.

Loving Attention

According to this principle, you can help your child channel her energies by conscientiously providing her with your loving attention. Your attention then becomes a kind of magnet drawing out your child's finer qualities and better behavior.

This method of guiding your child's behavior is called "Building," because it builds upon your child's sense of self-worth. In addition, it teaches your child that she does not have to misbehave to receive the attention and feeling of importance she craves. Your child receives the feeling of significance she needs without having to behave inappropriately to receive it.

Look For The Good

Parents feel hurt and frustrated when their child's behavior disappoints them. Children sense their parents' feelings and, consequently, feel worse about themselves. This, in turn, causes their behavior to decline.

Focus on your child's small but significant efforts and displays of responsibility. What you look for you will find. When you see your child's good behavior, you will feel better about your child and, in turn, be able to see more good behavior. The better you feel about your child, the better your child will behave.

Examples of Building

You will find it easy to use Building once you know how. Read the following examples to give you a better idea of how and when to use this technique.

- Johnny chased his sister around the house. His mother requested, "Please stop running in the house." He paused, and in that instant she turned to him and said, "Thank you for doing exactly what I asked."

- In an effort to be the constant center of attention, Amy commonly interrupted dinner-time conversations. One night, however, her father noticed Amy quietly eating while the grown-ups talked. Rather than waiting for her to interrupt before he gave her attention, he paused in his conversation, turned to Amy and said, "I really want to thank you for allowing us to speak without interruption. That shows real respect, consideration and patience. Very mature!"

- Without being asked, Brian hung his coat in the closet instead of tossing it on the couch. His mother showed him that she noticed and appreciated this effort by thanking him sincerely.

- Karen asked for a popsicle in a normal voice rather than using the whining tone she had been asked to eliminate from her speech. Her father recognized this and quickly responded, "You asked for something in your normal tone. What a big girl you are becoming. That was great. Thanks!"

When Building May Not Work

Building does not work if you shower your child with criticism and complaints on a fairly constant basis. Children who receive too much criticism cannot accept respect and approval, because they regard it as false and manipulative.

If you do not see your child's right action, you are not looking. *To some degree* your child always does a good job or behaves well. Something admirable, praise-worthy or special expresses itself through your child's personality on some level, to some degree, at all times. The more you look for this, the more you will see it. The more appreciation you allow yourself to express and experience for your child, the more effort your child will make to express herself at a higher level.

Applications Of Building

Whenever you find it necessary to correct your child's behavior, immediately follow with Building. This re-establishes a positive rapport between you and your child and protects you from falling into a critical habit. The child benefits, as well, by receiving positive support for her self-esteem, which may need a boost after hearing criticism of her behavior.

Try playing the "10 Times A Day" game with your child. It creates a positive atmosphere in the home and consistently reinforces your child's earnest efforts to do well. During the day, make a habit of viewing your child as sacred, valuable and important at least 10 times each day. Just stop and look at or think of her in a loving, accepting way. As part of your nightly ritual, remind your child that she is important, that her feelings count, and that she is precious just as she is.

Reverence: The Building Attitude

Practice *reverence* with your child. The feeling of reverence, while much like that of respect, runs deeper than respect. Reverence comes from recognition of your child's sacred nature and fills you with awe for that being. Focusing reverence upon a child reveals the child's magnificence and builds upon it.

Practicing Reverence means opening your heart to acknowledge, imagine and affirm the sacred spark, the hint of infinite being and pure divine perfection in your child's spirit. It means regarding your child as sacred, divine and perfect and regarding being with your child as a privilege.

When you practice reverence, a sense of holiness emanates from you and reaches your child. People intuitively sense and respond to how we feel and think about them, and children, who demonstrate far more openness and sensitivity than adults, receive and respond to our attitudes toward them most dramatically of all.

From time to time during the day, pause and look at your child or picture her in your mind's eye. Allow yourself to feel the deepest gratitude praise for this sacred gift with which God has blessed you.

◆

20

Natural Consequences

While older children learn from consequences, infants lack the capacity to learn from consequences lessons that they immediately can apply. A seven-month-old child, for example, will place her hand in a dish of ice water and keep it there even while the pain of the cold -- the negative consequence -- makes her cry. Remove her hand, warm it up, but keep the dish within reach, and she will place her hand back in the freezing water as soon as she gets a chance.

Pleasant consequences do not teach infants either, because they are too young to connect the pleasant consequence with their behavior. Just because you smile or cheer when your seven-month-old does something wonderful, she does not then seek to repeat her performance to achieve a repeat of your response.

A Strong-Willed Child

Some parents who are ignorant of their infant's age-related abilities and development presume they have a "strong-willed" child because he does not change his behavior in response to pain. For instance, they might use hitting to control a one-year-old, but a child of this age cannot draw the connection between the physical pain he receives and what he may have done to provoke it. The child only learns to treat himself and others as they treat him -- in this case, violently.

In fact, a child who receives excessively painful consequences frequently actually develops a diminished capacity to learn from consequences. In other words, even after she reaches the developmental stage when children normally recognize the connection between their actions and the consequences they experience, such a child will require excessively abusive consequences to learn

Self-Control

Children cannot always comply because *their own will* is not strong enough or developed enough. Your child may want to behave in a manner that causes you to respond positively, but he may still lack the self-control to do so. Children develop their power to comply by engaging in activity that demands their concentration and self-control. Provide your child of any age with opportunities to exercise the most self-discipline he can, and his power of self control will grow stronger. For example, as your two-and-a-half-year-old child concentrates and controls his body to perform a task, such as spooning peas from one bowl and into another, his control over his own body, emotions and intellect grows.

Observe Your Child's Ability

Your child may begin demonstrating to some degree the ability to change her behavior in response to consequences somewhere around 12 months of age. You may observe this ability sooner or later than this, and you may find that she demonstrates it in stages. In other words, in some instances your child may connect consequences with behavior while in other instances she may not.

Observe your child carefully to accurately assess her abilities in this area. Once you know your child has connected consequences with behavior, begin using consequences to guide her toward the behavior you want your child to demonstrate.

However, administering harsh or painful consequences to a child unable to respond to those consequences exhibits cruelty and ignorance.

Nature teaches all of us from consequences. Until your child demonstrates the capacity to learn from consequences, you have the responsibility to protect him from life's potentially harmful reactions to his actions. However, after he reaches the age where consequences serve as his teacher, you do your child a disservice by continuing to insulate him from life's educational experiences. In other words, let your child learn from life's consequences, or experience, whenever possible.

Letting Your Child Learn

Resist the urge to rescue your child from the natural consequences that bring out her more responsible potential. For instance, you might observe your five-year-old treating her friend poorly. Then, when her friend pulls your child's hair in retaliation, or elects not to play with your child, she learns what happens when she is not nice to others. She also learns to relate more amicably with other children.

You might, as another example, not stop your child from playing too roughly with a new toy, which causes it to break. Then, when he cries out for another and does not receive one, he learns to treat his toys more carefully.

One parent related to me the following story, which shows extremely well the importance of letting children learn from natural consequences: Ernest had been saving money for months to purchase a special, collector's baseball card. He even marked on his calendar the day he would have enough money to buy it. While out with his mother just one week before that day arrived, he spotted a new video game that he also wanted. His mother wanted to stop him from spending his money on impulse, but did not do so. She merely reminded him that he would not have the money to purchase the card for which he had been saving. He said he understood, but proceeded to spend the money anyway. When the day arrived when he would have been able to purchase the card but could not, he begged his parents to buy it for him. They wanted to, because he seemed so unhappy and disappointed. Instead, they controlled themselves and allowed their child to learn from the natural consequences of spending money on impulse.

Your Experience Of Your Child's Consequences

It takes inner strength to resist the temptation to rescue your child from the pain of doing without instant gratification. Doing so can make your life miserable in the short-run, because you suffer when your child feels unhappy, and her unhappiness may cause her to behave in a negative manner; your child might intentionally behave in disturbing ways in an effort to punish you for not satisfying her desire.

Your willingness to endure this unpleasantness in the short-run for a greater, more-lasting benefit defines your character and helps your child in two ways:

1. Your child learns directly from life's lessons (natural consequences), and
2. The experience demonstrates the use of self-restraint for a higher purpose.

Pause To Consider The Consequences

Instead of impulsively giving in to your child or automatically doing things to protect him from his own feelings or mistakes, pause to consider this question: "Would doing what I know is best for my child hamper him from doing what is best for himself?" Unless you find your child in a dangerous situation that obviously requires you to take protective action, temper your automatic impulse to help with a wiser, deeper view.

While hard to do, letting your child make "mistakes" teaches her responsibility and fosters self-reliance. When you take over your child's responsibilities by rescuing, reminding, pleading, and prodding her to do what you have asked or what she needs to do, you teach her that you, rather than she, are the one responsible for her responsibilities. Before involving yourself in your child's behavior, consider if she would be better off feeling the consequences of *not* being responsible than having you *make* her responsible. In some instances, nothing helps a child more than learning from the natural consequences of her actions.

Inciting Rebellion

Consistently, forcing your child to be responsible or to behave in a certain way backfires, and instead of compliance you receive rebellion. If your son forgets to bring his book bag into the car when you are ready to drive him to school, do not *automatically* remind him to bring it. He may resent your involvement even if it aims at protecting him from problems at school. He may see your reminders as simply babyish or bossy treatment rather than attempts to help.

Always regard your child's feelings as important. If you act as if having his book bag is more important to you than the way he feels about himself, your actions will incite his rebellion rather than encourage his responsibility. Of course, you can remind your child about his responsibilities from time to time. Be careful, though, how often you do so, because you may be encouraging him to become overly dependent upon you and others.

Before automatically rescuing your child, think about the outcome you want to achieve. Your child may become a happier, more responsible individual by having the freedom to learn from his own mistakes.

Removing The Safety Net

Seventeen-year-old Alex smashed his first car in a drag race he was not supposed to enter. For this action, his mother felt he needed the consequence of having to go without his own car. His father, however, bought him a new one, because

Alex promised he would do no more drag racing. The day he received the new car he entered another race and, this time, had a much more serious accident.

If you routinely rescue your child from the negative consequences of his actions, he may grow up expecting you always to act as his safety net. Considering that expectation, he might continually place himself in a situation where he needs you to save him. In the above example, the negative consequence of wrecking the car would have been to be without a car. Providing another car was a form of parental rescue, which obviously did not teach Alex to behave more responsibly with his automobile.

The next time you warn your child by saying, "You know, I won't always be there to protect you from your mistakes," ask yourself if your actions give her another message. Teach your child responsibility by giving her responsibility and by allowing her to take on that responsibility herself.

♦

21

Administering Consequences

Situations exist in which permitting your child to learn from the natural consequences of his behavior becomes an irresponsible, rather than a responsible, parental act. Sometimes you must devise and use a negative consequence to motivate your child to behave in safe or appropriate ways. Just about every child needs his parents to issue a negative consequence from time to time, and such consequences provide a clear and consistent message about expected behavior.

Restricting Privileges

Appropriate negative consequences consist of restricting your child's privileges. Never use losing your temper, reacting with anger or any form of intimidating, shaming, complaining, nagging, pleading, arguing, screaming, withdrawing your love, or violent behavior as a negative consequence. All of the above behaviors lower your child's self-confidence and self-esteem, increase her anger and unhappiness and make it harder for her to behave well.

The aim of a negative consequence should not be to make your child unhappy but to assist her in developing the self-control she needs to behave in more appropriate and considerate ways. Of course, for negative consequences to work, your child needs to be at the developmental stage when he can learn from consequences, as discussed in the previous chapter.

When Consequences Do Not Seem To Work

If you have had no success using unpleasant consequences to guide your child, the problem may lie in your choice of consequences or in how you use them. If consequences do not work, try using different ones.

Also, look closely at your child to discern if something other than negative consequences would work better. Some children simply need more understanding to improve their behavior, which you can offer through patient, loving discussions and more conscious, sensitive interventions. . Or, your child may simply need you to be more patient, more flexible, more willing to compromise with him. He may need you to give him more freedom and responsibility, more of an opportunity to do things his own way and to feel like a leader. Your child may need to feel more loved and valued as he is or more approval and appreciation for what he already does right.

Imposing a negative consequence will not work if your involvement constitutes intrusion, interference or overbearing control over your child's life. Children generally respond wonderfully to truly fair and reasonable treatment. If the consequences you impose do not feel fair and reasonable to your child, his misbehavior may be a form of rebellion against injustice.

The "I Don't Care" Response

When you tell your child you will apply a negative consequence if she continues behaving unacceptably, she may reply, "I don't care." This remark, commonly heard from many children in similar situations, has one of two likely meanings. First, your child may actually be feeling that you do not truly care about her, because you either refuse to listen to her point of view or you exhibit too little consideration for her feelings. Second, your child may be using this response as a tactic aimed at discouraging your efforts to be in charge.

Pause to consider your child's actual feelings when you receive this response. Try giving her a statement that lets her know you understand and care about her feelings. For example, if your child screams to be taken to the pool, the consequence for your child's behavior might be losing the privilege of going to the pool. You might say, "I understand that you really want to go to the pool right now, but your screaming is not the way to make that happen." Showing your child that you love her as you demonstrate strength brings out more compliance and helps to preserve her self-respect.

However, do not be manipulated by your child's obvious attempt to make you feel powerless and defeated. Register the "I don't care" response without reacting fearfully and without automatically threatening more severe consequences. See what actually happens when you follow through with the consequence.

List Your Child's Privileges

Parents sometimes experience difficulty devising consequences that work. If you have this problem, solve it by making a list of your child's privileges. You can then refer to this list when looking for an appropriate consequence to apply.

For example, the list might include the little things that your child likes to do or to have, such as playing Nintendo, watching television, going to the pool, playing with a particular stuffed animal or doll, telephone or car privileges, going to special events, having ice cream or popsicles, or playing with a particular friend. Do not include things essential to his well being and development, such as receiving hugs and kisses, playing with his father, reading, or being treated as a worthwhile human being.

When you begin this list, you might have difficulty thinking of things about which your child really cares. In this case, observe your child more closely and take note of his activities, preferences and requests. He may want to eat candy, watch videos, stay up late, or play in the parked car. If your child is older, he might want to be driven to the mall. To have these privileges he must earn them through appropriate, responsible, respectful behavior that you know he is capable of demonstrating.

Make your list as long as you can, and, when you feel the need to issue a consequence, choose a privilege from the list and restrict it. You might want to try giving your child the chance to choose his own consequence from the list instead of you making the consequence decision. Give him 15 seconds to make his choice. If he does not make the choice in the allotted time, choose for him.

You might include time limits on your list. Decide beforehand how long to restrict a given privilege. Generally, avoid imposing restrictions that last longer than one week. If additional consequences become necessary, rather than adding more time to a previous consequence simply increase the number of privileges you restrict.

Experiment with lighter restrictions first. Younger children cannot stand delayed gratification. Therefore, just warning your child that if he continues whining he will have to wait five extra minutes before you allow him to watch cartoons can motivate him to quiet down and walk away.

The Consequence That Works

Look for consequences that matter most to your child. Using logical and immediate consequences is advisable; however, finding consequences that work represents the bottom line. Logical consequences are those that work in the following manner: If your child oversteps her boundaries, she has less freedom; if she over-indulges, she forfeits an indulgence.

Find your child's favorite privilege, and then use it as a warning for all sorts of things. For instance, if your child chooses staying up late over any other activity, warn him that if he does not do as you say you will reduce his bedtime by 15 minutes as a consequence.

Following Through

When your child's inappropriate behavior meets with no consequences, she receives an unclear and inconsistent message about what you expect of her, which can confuse her. However, many parents find it too painful or difficult to follow through on consequences. By not doing so, they guarantee that their children routinely will disregard their warnings, rules, requests, and directions.

If you have this problem, start exercising small degrees of self-discipline in this area. Rescue *a little less* and issue *easy-to-implement* consequences. Even though the consequence might seem too slight to matter much, the practice of following through on them will begin to develop the strength you need to be more firm. In the process, you teach your child that you do what you say you will do, which may act as a deterrent for her misbehavior.

Take Your Time

Believing you must quickly decide on a consequence can result in difficulty following through. When you feel rushed, angry or upset, delay making a decision about what consequence to apply. Anger befuddles our thinking and causes us to overreact. Take your time making the decision. Simply tell your child there will be a consequence if he does not change his behavior. Then let him know later, after you have had the chance to calm down and think of a consequence on which you can follow through, what consequence you have decided to implement.

You Can Change Your Mind

Do not feel stuck with the consequence you choose. Disciplining a child does not require you to function like an inflexible, inhuman symbol of absolute authority. As a fallible, learning, growing human being, you need to permit yourself to change your mind when new facts surface or a new point of view becomes apparent. This sets an honest, natural example for your child.

After issuing a consequence, you might rethink your decision and discover a better idea about what will work for your child or what would be more fair and reasonable. Go ahead and use the best idea you have. If, upon rethinking, you feel it would have been best not to have issued a consequence at all, let your child know you have changed your mind. You do not have to do something just because you said you would if wisdom dictates a change of course.

Explaining The System

Begin using a consequence system with children as young as 18 months. If your child is three or over, explain the consequence system before using it. You can introduce her to the system by involving her in the privilege list-making process. You may find yourself surprised at how willingly she talks about herself when you say, "Help me make a list of the things you like to do. The items on this list will be things you will have to lose for a time when you misbehave." Children thrive on clear definitions of rules. They see these rules as a positive challenge to meet and treat them quite seriously.

Guidelines For Application

To successfully administer consequences, use the following guidelines:

1. ***Strictly apply the measures of self-control you learned in the first part of this book.*** If you express much anger or stress to your child, you undermine your authority and diminish the effectiveness of any negative consequences you might impose. Your angry response to your child triggers his anger and resentment. Remember the three-part formula for parenting effectiveness: peace, poise and power. When you lose your peace and poise, you lose your power to effectively guide your child's behavior.

2. ***Provide your child with a steady base of unconditional love and sensitive respect for his feelings.***

3. ***Apply Conscious Detachment to avoid making too much of your child's misbehavior.*** Provide your child with plenty of Building to teach her that she can receive the attention and sense of importance she needs without misbehaving.

4. ***Eliminate angry criticism of your child.*** Remember that your child accepts the self-image you define for him through your verbal labels and then acts according to that self-image.

5. ***Carefully monitor your behavior to provide your child with a consistent demonstration of appropriate, respectful, responsible behavior.*** Based on The Law of Reflection, children give back the behavior they receive.

6. ***Carefully construct your child's environment and routine.*** Providing your child with order and harmony in her surroundings and an orderly, regular, unrushed routine brings out your child's orderly behavior.

7. ***Avoid over-controlling your child.*** Create environments in which your young child can play freely with minimal parental control and assistance.

8. ***Do not rescue your child at the expense of his opportunity to become more responsible for himself.***

9. ***Be fair and reasonable with your child.***

10. ***Make time for calm and loving closeness with your child.***

Let The Consequences Work

When you begin using consequences, your child may disregard your warnings and continue behaving poorly even after you have implemented a consequence. Therefore, you may be tempted to presume that consequences do not work and prematurely abandon the system, which is just what your child probably hoped would happen if he disregarded your warnings and the subsequent consequences.

Do not be discouraged if your child chooses to ignore your warnings. Simply follow through at least 90 percent of the time. Give the consequences a chance to work. If you consistently follow the guidelines in this chapter, nine out of 10 times your child will respond to your warning or simply heed your rules.

◆

22

The 1-2-3 Warning System

As a general rule, prior to applying a consequence to your child's misbehavior, warn him that you will do so should he continue misbehaving. Consistently give your child the same number of warnings and present them in the same way. This makes your warnings most effective.

The 1-2-3 Warning System

The "1-2-3 Warning System" provides a simple way to warn your child consistently and effectively. By giving your child two warnings and imposing a consequence when he misbehaves a third time, you give him the time he needs to gain control over his own behavior in a reasonably patient and tolerant manner.

Jumping from a single warning right into issuing a consequence overlooks the "physics" of child behavior. Like a speeding car, your child's behavior has momentum and force behind it, and he needs time to get this under control. Only then can he do what you ask.

Giving your child two chances to correct his behavior or comply with your request not only makes it easier for him to gain control of himself, it also makes the process easier on you. You will not have to administer consequences as frequently, because, if you apply this system correctly, your child will change his behavior following your first or second warning at least 90 percent of the time.

When To Start

The 1-2-3 Warning System has proven most effective for children between two and 12 years of age. It works with all sorts of behavior problems. Implement it to stop your child's whining, nagging, arguing, shouting, sibling rivalry, non-compliance, tantrums, and disrespect. For children over 12, you should still give them two chances when possible. (You do not have to count aloud or show your fingers; see below.)

When you start using this system, let your child know beforehand that you are going to use it, and tell him how it works. For children under 12, you could use the following simple explanation: "From now on, when I ask or tell you to do something or to stop doing something, I will give you a few seconds to comply. If you don't, I will start counting with the number one. If I reach three, you receive a consequence."

Remember, for this system, or for any other child discipline system, to work effectively, you need to maintain your emotional balance -- your peace, poise and power -- in response to your child's misbehavior. If you exhibit much anger or stress, your child may feel it is worth receiving a consequence just to make you miserable for not letting her be in charge.

How To Use The 1-2-3 Warning System

For the 1-2-3 Warning System to work effectively, use it in the following manner:

1. **When your child does not comply, start counting.** When you ask or direct your child to do something or to stop behaving in a particular manner and he does not comply, start counting with the number one. When you first begin using this system, you might add, "If I reach three, you have a consequence." If you know what the consequence will be, you can tell your child at that time.

2. ***Clearly and firmly state AND show the count.*** State the number clearly by saying, "That's one," as you hold up one finger to show your count. It is crucial to show the count with your fingers as you state it clearly and firmly. Using visual *and* verbal cues together impacts your child more strongly than using verbal cues alone.

3. ***Give your child five seconds to comply.*** If she does not, proceed to the count of two by saying firmly, "That's two," and hold up two fingers.

4. ***Use Building.*** When your child complies before you reach three, respond positively by praising and thanking him.

5. ***If your child stops misbehaving at the count of one or two and then misbehaves again within 15 minutes, advance numerically from where you left off.*** For instance, if she stops speaking disrespectfully after you count one, respond with Building. If she then engages in another form of misbehavior, or if she repeats the same misbehavior, within 15 minutes, begin your count at two. If your child stops again but within 15 minutes misbehaves again, immediately say, "That's three," and give her a consequence.

6. ***Follow through.*** For your count to be effective, consistently follow through and issue a consequence if you reach the count of three. If you fail to follow through on a consistent basis, your child will defy you consistently and with impunity. *If you consistently follow through, your child soon will respond positively to the count of one or two at least 90 percent of the time.*

7. ***Start "fresh" after reaching the count of three and imposing a consequence, and do not talk about the event right away.*** After you reach the count of three, inform your child that he has a consequence, then let the matter go. Be loving and start "fresh," as if nothing had happened. Allow the consequence to do the work of motivating your child to change. After receiving a consequence, your child needs to know that you love him and respect the way he feels. Do not immediately attempt to explain why you had to administer a consequence, because it may turn into a stressful argument that will undermine your authority and dissipate the effectiveness of the system. Save this discussion for a later time.

8. ***You do not need to know the consequence when you start counting.*** If your child asks you what the consequence will be when you begin to count, simply say, "I'll let you know." Give yourself the time you need to think about it, and inform her when you are ready. When you finally do inform her of the consequence, be sure to remind her of what she did to earn it.

9. ***If your child's behavior worsens, begin the process again.*** If your child reacts with a tantrum when you reach the count of three, try overlooking it with Conscious Detachment for a while. If the tantrum continues, start counting again, and tell him that he needs to either settle down or time himself out to a designated area (Do not tell or treat the child as if her rage or unhappiness is wrong or bad, only that imposing this behavior upon others represents disrespect. This type of expression in private demonstrates respect for one's own feelings as well as the feelings of others). Let the time out last until he settles down, or you can use a timer and let it last about one minute per year of life. Or you can tell him that, if you reach three this time, the time of the consequence he is angry about will be extended or an additional consequence will be imposed.

For example, your child whines for a candy bar for breakfast. You refuse and she continues. You start counting with the warning, "If I reach three before you stop whining, you will not be allowed any candy at all for the entire day," but she continues. When you reach three, you tell her that now she will not have any candy today. In reaction to this, she throws a tantrum. You tell her either to stop the tantrum or to take it in her room. She ignores you, so you start counting again, and warn, "If I reach three, there will be no candy tomorrow either." If you reach three, follow through. Any time she asks for candy that day, say something like, "Normally I might allow you to have it, but, because you refused to throw your tantrum in the appropriate place this morning, you get no candy today.

Sometimes Warnings Are Impractical Or Unsafe

Obviously, it will not always be practical, possible or safe to issue warnings. When your child's action endangers her or someone else, you need to stop her right away. When she misbehaves in a manner too extreme for warnings, abandon the warning system. However, nine times out of 10, issuing warnings will be appropriate. If you overrule the warning system too often, it loses its impact.

♦

23

Pre-Arranged Consequences

Some parents feel uncomfortable or have difficulty coming up with consequences for their children's misbehavior. If you feel this way, the "Pre-Arranged Consequence System" may make this task easier. Using the Pre-Arranged Consequence System involves combining the list of your child's privileges with a list of consequences for particular misbehaviors.

To use this system, you first must make a list composed of your child's most frustrating behaviors. This list might include behaviors such as whining, not sleeping in his own bed through the night, not coming when called, making you wait for him longer than necessary, ignoring you when you speak to him, talking back disrespectfully, arguing, not picking up after himself, refusing to do his homework, throwing tantrums, or hitting.

After you have made this list, write a consequence next to each misbehavior. This consequence will result when your child behaves in the manner described. For instance, your list might look like this:

Misbehavior	**Consequence**
Talking back disrespectfully	Lose 30 minutes of TV time
Whining for what you want	The privilege of having it is denied
Not doing homework without being told	Loss of all play privileges until it's done

Misbehavior	**Consequence**
Throwing a tantrum (outside of a place where a tantrum is permitted)	Lose privilege of going to the swimming pool
Resisting bedtime	Reduction or loss of story time that night

The Consequences

The consequences you choose for your list do not have to demonstrate a direct, logical connection to your child's behavior. Also, you may involve your child in the writing of both lists. Children often come up with excellent consequences for themselves and remember misbehaviors you might otherwise have forgotten to include on the list. Many children regard the consequence system as a fair and reasonable way of dealing with their behavior, and they appreciate its clarity and predictability.

A modified version simply involves creating a list of the behaviors you disallow and for which there will be negative consequences. You do not have to decide on the consequences in advance. Wait until your child breaks the rules to come up with the consequence.

You can begin using this system effectively for children around the time they turn two, and continue using it through the child's teenage years. As your child matures, update the lists of his privileges, behaviors and consequences.

How This System Works

Allow your child to see the list of disallowed behavior (and the list of consequences if you have one) in advance, so that she knows beforehand what you expect from her and what she can expect when she breaks the rules. Then, use the

1-2-3 Warning System and, if you already know what the consequence will be, begin your count with a reminder of the pre-arranged consequence that follows if you reach three.

Compose A Positive List

The Pre-Arranged Consequence System works best when you combine it with a third list made up of the positive behaviors you want your child to exhibit. To assist you in composing this list, look at the descriptions of your child's frustrating behaviors and change each into a description of the behavior you want in its place. For instance, you might change "talking back disrespectfully" into "speaking to me with respect"; "arguing with me" into "complying without an argument"; "not picking up after yourself" into "placing things back where they belong when you are done with them"; "throwing tantrums" into "keeping your composure when you do not get your way."

Then, watch for times when your child exhibits these positive behaviors and recognize him with Building responses of praise and thanks.

The Sticker-Chart Building Method

A more demonstrable way of using the list of positive behaviors involves turning it into a chart. When your child behaves in one of the ways described in the list, he receives a sticker, such as a star. Let him place the sticker on the chart if he likes.

Make the receiving of stickers a regular part of the nightly ritual or give the sticker spontaneously, whatever works for you. Each time you award him a sticker, express your delight in his accomplishment. Place the chart where he can see it.

When the child has earned 20 stickers, she can then receive a special treat, such as an outing to her favorite fast-food restaurant or a new accessory for a doll. Some parents require the child to earn fewer stickers for her reward, but if you accept less than 10 the system may not work. This system works, because by the time the child receives her special reward she has developed a lasting pattern of improved behavior. The sticker system has proven effective in many households and classrooms for children under 12 and over two.

◆

24

Spontaneous Consequences

Another way of using consequences to guide your child's behavior frees you from having to come up with a consequence on the spot. This method, called "The Spontaneous Consequence System," can be applied in two ways: with and without warnings.

When used in conjunction with the 1-2-3 Warning System, simply inform the child she has a consequence when you reach three, but do not tell her what it will be. Later, when you see her about to do something she likes or when she wants something, use that opportunity as the consequence for her previous misbehavior. When issuing the consequence, remind your child of exactly what she did earlier to receive it.

An Example of Spontaneous Consequences

Let us say that in an angry reaction to not getting his way, your seven year old throws a pillow from the couch across the living room. You tell him that throwing things constitutes inappropriate behavior, and, holding up a finger, you state, "That's one." Still angry, he ignores the warning and throws another pillow. You count, "That's two." He throws another pillow, and you reach the count of three. To use the Spontaneous Consequence System here, you would maintain your composure and calmly inform him that he has earned a consequence, even though you do not yet know what it will be.

A short while later, your child asks for permission to go outside to play with his friends. Seizing your opportunity, you say, "Remember earlier when you threw the pillows, and I counted to three? I know that when we feel angry it is hard to control ourselves, but you know that is inappropriate behavior. You need to exercise better self-control. As a consequence, you are not permitted to go out to play with your friends for one hour."

If The Child Apologizes Or Argues

At the point when you actually impose the consequence, your child may apologize for his earlier behavior. Accept his apology graciously, and tell him you appreciate it, but the consequence must stand because he continued his misbehavior for the count of three.

If he begins to argue with you and complain that you are being unfair, do not argue back. If he wants to discuss the matter, tell him that you will discuss it at another time. Discussions conducted when you want compliance or when you issue a consequence virtually always result in a waste of your energy, an increase in your stress level and a much greater likelihood that your conflict with your child will grow uglier and more intense.

If the child persists in arguing or nagging, or if he begins acting out his anger in another form of misbehavior, try ignoring it (if that seems reasonable). Otherwise, begin counting again for another consequence.

Without Warning

Instances occur in which issuing a warning or informing your child that she has just earned a consequence may not be possible, because the child's behavior may be too serious for a warning. For instance, if she steals something, hurts someone, or destroys another's property, your child has gone too far for a warning. Your child may do something, and then run off before you have the chance to tell her that she has earned a consequence. She might misbehave in a public setting where you feel it would be better to say nothing and to avoid making any further scene at the time.

In situations like these, issue a Spontaneous Consequence later, without warning. You do not have to think up a consequence. Observe your child's actions. When she wants to engage in an activity for pleasure, or when she asks you for permission or for a favor, use not granting her wishes as the consequence. If your child exhibited extremely serious behavior, you may do this a few times as a multiple consequence for a single act.

Example Of A Spontaneous Consequence Without Warning

Let us say that you take your child to a school function being held in the cafeteria. For no apparent reason other than, perhaps, to prove that he can get away with it, he decides to jump up on one of the table tops and dance on it for about five seconds. Before you can do or say anything he returns to his seat. Your better judgment advises you to say and do nothing about it for now, even if it means that your child thinks he got away with that behavior for the time being.

On your drive home together after the school function, he reminds you that you promised to stop for ice cream. You use this as your opportunity for a Spontaneous Consequence, which you then issue by saying, "Remember when you danced on the table in the cafeteria.. You know that was inappropriate. The consequence for dancing on the table is that we do not stop for ice cream today."

Your Child Will Not Like It

When you impose a consequence in this manner, your child probably will not nod in pleasant agreement and say, "Yes, I see what you mean. I certainly do deserve this

consequence.   Thank you for helping me to do better."
Instead, using the above example again, he might scream out,
"But you promised!"

You do not have to argue or explain. Your reasons are
obvious. He knows that what he did was out of line. Do not
engage in a stressful, pointless argument in which you try to
explain what he already understands.

A Strategic Pause

It usually pays to strategize before you respond to any
situation, and responding to your child is no different. In fact,
your best strategy almost always involves waiting until you have
calmed down and had some time to think before responding.
Do not strain yourself with the effort to come up with instant
solutions to problems.

Using Spontaneous Consequences gives you time to
think before taking action. You can wait hours before issuing a
Spontaneous Consequence. An impulsive, emotional trigger
reaction to your child's behavior rarely constitutes a careful,
accurate, constructive response based on a clear view of the
facts.

Consequences, Not Cruelty

When you issue a Spontaneous Consequence, do not be
vindictive about it. Consequences become cruel and counter
productive when applied with a spiteful, antagonistic or
competitive attitude or in a way aimed at making your child feel
angry, hurt or distressed.

Your child may show no apparent remorse or concern
when you issue the consequence. Do not let this antagonize
you to impose more consequences or react with anger.
Maintain your peace and poise and you preserve your authority,
because you can think clearly and respond intelligently from

that base. Give the consequence a chance to work, and know that it works when your child's behavior improves, not when she feels inferior or unhappy.

Minor Consequences

A Spontaneous Consequence, then, consists of anything you withhold from your child spontaneously, without planning, when the opportunity presents itself in an effort to deter a specific negative behavior. A Spontaneous Consequence need not be large to work nor have any direct logical connection to the child's form of misbehavior. In fact, even small or minor Spontaneous Consequences work well.

For instance, if your child runs through church after being clearly told to behave in a quieter and more orderly manner, you may tell him that he has earned a consequence after he ignores your second warning. Later, when you arrive home, he may pop in his favorite video game and start playing. You see your opportunity, and say to him, "I know that you need to run free, and that it is hard to wait for the right time and place for that. However, running through church is disrespectful, and you disregarded my warnings. Your consequence for this is no video game for 15 minutes." If he nags you to let him play the game before the time is up, ignore it as long as you can or as long as it seems reasonable. If that does not work, use the 1-2-3 Warning System, and tell him the consequence of his continued behavior will be an additional five minutes of waiting to play the game.

The consequence of merely 15 or 20 minutes of delayed gratification may seem small to you, and your child may say that she does not care. However, to a child, any delay seems endless and hard to bear. A brief delay in her gratification can prove to be a sufficiently severe Spontaneous Consequence, and one on which you easily can follow through.

◆

25

Time Out

Most parents, teachers and caregivers know about and use a consequence called "Time Out." The Time Out consequence consists of restricting your child's privilege of "space" as a result of the child's inappropriate behavior within a particular space. For instance, if your child plays too aggressively in a room where he might break something or where his play demonstrates disrespect for the other people in the room, he may be "Timed Out" of that room, or Timed Out to a particular seat in the room or to a particular part of the room, as a consequence. When used correctly, Time Out serves as an effective means of encouraging a child's self-discipline without having a negative impact on the child's self-esteem.

When To Use Time Out

When used in conjunction with the 1-2-3 Warning System, Time Outs have worked extremely well as a method for stopping a child's whining, nagging, arguing, disrespect, screaming, hitting, tantrums, and sibling rivalry. You can use Time Out when you and your child are home and when you are out. You can use it with one child or with more than one child at a time.

Time Out, as described in this chapter, has worked with children as young as 18 months and as old as 12. Teens demonstrate a willingness to time themselves out when they feel frustrated, which is exactly what you want them to do. Time Out provides them with the appropriate space to regain their self-control.

Is Time Out For Your Child?

Not all parenting tips or techniques work for all parents or all children. It may be that your child does not need Time Out or that he responds better to other kinds of consequences. Observe your child and consider using other options if you do not like the results you achieve when using Time Out.

If you have tried using Time Out without satisfaction, before giving up on the method take a good look at the following guidelines and see if you have missed one or more of them in your approach. If so, try using Time Out again with these guidelines in mind, and see if this consequence works more effectively with your child than before.

How To Use Time Out

The basic guidelines for using Time Out effectively include:

1. ***Be firm, yet calm.*** As in the application of any other worthwhile approach to child discipline, use Time Out *without* anger, arguing, nagging, criticizing, complaining, pleading, screaming, or hitting. Maintain your peace, poise and power.

2. ***Consistently use the 1-2-3 Warning System before implementing a Time Out.*** When you intend to use Time Out as a consequence, tell your child this when you start counting. Say, "That's enough whining. That's one. If I reach three, you will have a Time Out."

3. ***Use Building in response to compliance.*** If your child complies at the count of one or two, praise and thank him for that behavior. If you reach the count of three and send your child to his Time Out place, thank him for compliance when he goes. As he heads off, you might say, "Thank you for listening to me and going to your room. I really appreciate that."

4. ***If your child continues to misbehave, warn him that he might have more consequences.*** If your child continues to misbehave on the way to his Time Out place, give him one warning and say, "If you continue acting out this way your Time Out will be lengthened." Consider also the option of simply overlooking this behavior as long as he goes to his prescribed Time Out place.

5. ***If your child refuses to go to the Time Out Place, warn her that she might have more consequences.*** If your child refuses to go to her Time Out place on her own, give her a warning that she will receive more time there if she does not comply. You may want simply to give her the choice of going on her own or being carried there by you. If you lack the physical strength to carry your child, or if you fear that controlling her physically might escalate into more conflict, do not try to force her to go. Tell her she has earned other consequences for this defiance. Time Out *yourself* at this point so you can calm down and center yourself. Then, review your child's list of privileges, or consider one or more of the consequence options described in the following chapter. Do *not* resort to the use of negative control tactics, such as shouting, losing your temper, arguing, pleading, or hitting to compel her compliance.

6. ***What to allow your child to do during Time Out at home.*** You may be surprised to find that allowing your child during Time Out to do as he pleases so long as he remains in the Time Out place accomplishes an improvement in his behavior. The separation or restriction of his "space privilege" proves to be sufficient for many children. To make the Time Out more severe, many combine the consequence of space restriction with not permitting the child to do anything at all during the Time Out, but this may express your anger and frustration rather than your love and wisdom. Experiment with varying degrees of sternness to find what works best for you and your child. For instance, you might only permit your child to read or write during Time Out. Try your best to *not* make the Time Out harsher than it needs to be, or, like any consequence, it will likely back-fire.

7. ***Use the appropriate length of Time Out.*** Time Out should last about one minute per year of a child's life. If you have to lengthen the Time Out because your child continues misbehaving, consider doubling it or adding an additional five minutes. Making a Time Out last for hours tends to increase a child's anger and her desire to rebel. Some parents are satisfied with the results achieved when they direct their children to remain in the Time Out place until they feel ready to behave appropriately. Try the option that suits you and your child best. If one fails, try the other. If you choose to assign a specific time limit, use a timer with a ringer on it that you place outside the child's Time Out place but within his earshot. Let the ringer, rather than you, inform her of when the Time Out has ended. You can then ignore her when she calls out, "Is it over yet?" Using a timer also helps you avoid unintentionally forcing your child to stay in her Time Out place too long when you forget she is there.

8. ***Choose a specific place at home to Time Out your child.*** At home, your child's bedroom serves as the best place for a Time Out. However, if this proves impossible or impractical for you, choose some other place. Definitely do *not* force the child to remain in a dark, frightening place or confine your child to a closet; these are cruel and damaging to your child's psyche. You also can make Time Out a "tag-along-in-silence" exercise, in which your child has to stay by your side without talking for a period of time as you go about your activities. You can also use a particular chair or corner where the child must remain for the duration of the Time Out.

9. ***Use Time Out to deal with tantrums.*** While your child throws a tantrum, he may not be aware that you have begun counting. Do not raise your voice to be heard. Count in your firm, but unstrained, voice and hold up your fingers in the normal manner. When you reach three, send him to his Time Out place. If he does not respond to your direction, carry him there and leave him alone without trying to calm him with reasoning. (If you cannot carry him for some reason, refer to the guideline above.)

10. ***If your child does not want to leave the Time Out place, let her stay.*** At the end of the Time Out, if your child wants to remain where she is, or if she falls asleep, make no effort to force her out. Instead, make the most of your free time. If you need to have her out of Time Out for some reason, direct her to leave and, if she does not comply, start counting for another consequence. (Obviously, if you need to go somewhere, administering a Time Out to be served at that time would not be an adequate consequence for stalling.)

11. ***If your child leaves Time Out early, send or take him
    back.*** When you do so, be sure to state that you will start
    the timer again. If he leaves again, repeat this procedure
    this time adding the warning that you will close the door (if
    Time Out is in his room) for the duration of the Time Out
    if he leaves early again. If he leaves early a third time,
    return him to the Time Out place and follow through on
    your warning. You can either close his door or have him
    close it. If the child normally closes the door, or if he likes
    the door closed, move on to the next step. If your child
    leaves after his door has been closed, return him once again
    (remaining calm but firm), re-start the timer, and this time
    say to him, "If you leave early again, the door will be locked
    for the duration of the Time Out." If you need to install a
    lock, install one that locks on the outside only. If your child
    then tests you, follow through. In all likelihood you will not
    need to use the lock more than once. One variation to
    closing and locking the door, which can be used if you have
    not chosen your child's room as the Time Out location,
    involves the following: Wherever your child's Time Out
    place happens to be, when he leaves early, return him to the
    Time Out place and re-start the timer. Simply do this as
    many times as you have to until he remains for the
    duration. If you remain calm, patient but firm and
    persistent, he eventually will get the message. Feel free to
    experiment with either variation to determine which works
    best for you. If you have more than one child, do not be
    surprised if the variation that works best for one proves to
    be less successful with another. Use the methods that work
    best for each individual child.

12. ***If your child throws a tantrum during her Time Out,
    ignore her antics.*** If your child screams, cries, crashes
    about, or even breaks things during her Time Out, do your
    best to ignore her behavior. When she sees she cannot
    control you in this manner, she will be less prone to resort

to this behavior next time. Do not repeatedly call into her room in an effort to calm down your child, and do not waste your effort using reason with a child in an emotional state; to do so will increase an already-tense situation.

13. ***If your child creates havoc in his room, let him live with the mess he creates.*** Rarely will a child wreck his room in a rage during his Time Out, but occasionally this does happen. Obviously, the child's aim in doing so either is to punish or to intimidate the person who sent him to the Time Out. (Or, you may need to teach him how to harmlessly punch his mattress and scream into a pillow to get his rage out of his system.). Do not react, and, thereby, encourage, this kind of behavior by allowing it to affect your emotional calm. Maintain your peace, poise and power. Let him live in the mess he has created until he cleans it himself. If he does not clean it up on his own, wait at least a day before you say anything about it. In so doing, you allow him to experience the natural consequence of either living in his own mess or of cleaning it up himself. If you deal with the mess too soon you may inadvertently extend or rekindle the original conflict. Wait until emotions have settled into neutral, and your direction for your child to clean his room will not be perceived as a negative reaction to his behavior. If he refuses to comply with your direction to clean his room, remain calm. Maintain the attitude that his misbehavior does not victimize you, it merely makes things harder on him. Begin counting for a consequence. (For children under five, you may have to get involved with the clean up to at least get them started. If you help with the clean up, let the child do as much of the work as possible.)

14. ***Do not immediately discuss the cause of the Time Out.*** While emotional tensions remain high, do not make the mistake of choosing to discuss with your child the inappropriateness of the behavior that forced you to

administer a consequence, warning or direction. To do so
will only trigger an argument or prolong the tension caused
by the conflict. After the Time Out has ended, do not
apologize for having to administer the Time Out or attempt
to explain yourself. Do not insist that the child show
remorse for or understanding of what he did to bring about
his consequence. Simply start fresh, seemingly forgetting
about the misbehavior and need for consequences, thereby
allowing his experience to teach him. Save discussions for a
later time when the combativeness of the situation has
passed and emotions are calm enough for reason.

15. **Demonstrate your love and use Building after
imposing a Time Out.** Immediately after the Time Out
(or after administering any other consequence or following
any warning), make a positive demonstration of your basic,
underlying love, appreciation and respect for your child.
Watch your child for good behavior, and use Building as
quickly as possible to point out at least two things she does
right or two qualities you appreciate or admire about her.
This neutralizes any resentment caused by the imposed
consequence and allows the two of you to begin relating in
a more positive manner once again. It also reinforces your
child's basic sense of self worth, without which her self-
esteem and her ability to behave well fall to lower levels.

16. **Time Out your child even when you are away from
home.** When away from home, you can use any space at
hand for a Time out. In a public place, you may have to
stay with your child during the Time Out, or at least keep
him in your view. If the child misbehaves while you dine in
a restaurant, the Time Out can consist of you escorting him
outside, where he must stand or sit with you for the
designated time. (You also can warn him that if he receives
another Time Out you will leave him home with a baby
sitter next time.) In a store, you may have to stand with

him for a few minutes in a corner or take him outside. In the car, a Time Out can be a period of enforced silence, or you might pull over and stop the car (when safe to do so); the child then must stay in the car for the duration of the Time Out while you wait outside.

17. *If your child misbehaves during religious services, impose a Time Out outside the sanctuary.* If your child misbehaves during a religious service, out of respect for the other people present and for the sacredness of the environment, give her a Time Out outside that environment. You may have to leave with your child. If that seems to be what the child wants, or if you do not want to be interrupted from your worship in this way, you may need to reconsider bringing her with you until she is older. It might be best to provide her with the religious education you want for her in your home at least for now.

18. *In the beginning, be willing to use Time Out repeatedly.* When you begin using Time Out, your child may behave in ways that cause you to send him to his room repeatedly in a single day. Be persistent through this testing period. As long as he cooperates at the count of three, you will not have to put up with his misbehavior for more than 10 or 15 seconds at a time. Once he realizes that his misbehavior consistently sends him to Time Out, he will stop testing.

19. *If Time Out does not seem to be working initially, use it for at least two weeks before abandoning this consequence.* Give Time Out a fair try before you abandon it, and be sure to follow the guidelines described in this chapter before deciding it does not work for your child. Use it for at least two weeks, and if, after that, you still feel dissatisfied with the results, you might restrict one of the child's other privileges instead.

20. **Use the Time Out with siblings and your child's friends.** If your children or their friends play or argue too aggressively, start counting for both of them. Say something like, "That's enough kids. You need to quiet down. That's one. If I reach three, you'll be Timed Out to separate places." If you reach three, follow through. If your child's friend misbehaves in your home, explain the 1-2-3 Warning System and tell her that she will receive a Time Out if you reach three. However, be sure to obtain her parents' permission first. If they refuse, consider not allowing their child to play in your home if she consistently behaves inappropriately.

21. **Give yourself a Time Out.** When you lose your self-control, give yourself a Time Out to cool off. In doing so, you teach your child what to do when he loses his self-control. When you give yourself a Time Out, avoid blaming your child for the way you feel.

◆

26

Handling Your Child's Reactions To Discipline

One factor more than any other prevents parents from establishing appropriate parameters for their children's behavior and from issuing negative consequences when their children go too far. Simply stated, they have difficulty handling their children's response to enforced parameters and consequences.

Your child's reaction to your efforts to discipline can be so outrageous that you may choose the *apparently* easier option of ceasing to make that effort. Your decision to stop disciplining your child, of course, represents exactly what your child hoped to achieve with his disturbing behavior.

Children Need Firmness With Love

Doing more than you should to keep your child happy may save you from enduring your child's pouting or shouting. However, in the long run, behaving in this manner intensifies the problems with your child and causes your child's behavior to worsen. The reason for this is simple: Children depend upon their parents to help them define clear, firm, consistent behavioral boundaries.

We usually think of firmness as unloving and permissiveness as loving, but this belief can be inaccurate. The right measure of firmness, strength, discipline, and restraint provide essential qualities for actualizing the higher potential of any relationship, including your relationship with your child. When parental leniency becomes excessive, it expresses weakness in the parent and fosters weakness in the child.

Disciplinary Actions

Parental disciplinary action includes four basic actions you must take to support your child's positive behavioral development.

- Refuse to be manipulated or controlled by your child's demands. For instance, do not automatically rush to her just because she cries for you or wants you to come;
- Resist the urge to compulsively rescue your child from dealing with difficulty or from independent struggle;
- Allow your child to make some of his own mistakes so he can learn from the unpleasant natural consequences he brings upon himself;
- Establish clear and consistent rules, and issue and follow through on consequences that enforce these rules.

All four of these actions require a certain measure of parental *self*-discipline to administer.

Testing

Taking firm, disciplinary action sometimes elicits even worse behavior from your child. This behavior may be a negative reaction aimed at discouraging you from asserting your power in the relationship. However, if you remain firm through this testing period, your child learns that her negative control tactics do not work, and the value of this lesson is enormous.

The earlier your child learns that her negative control tactics and inappropriate, irresponsible, disrespectful behavior produce negative results, the sooner she begins working on developing more positive ways of achieving her desired results. Teaching your child this lesson serves as one of your essential parental functions. If your child does not learn this from your reactions to her actions, she goes out into the world with the expectation that the behavior that worked with you will work for her in all situations.

When Is Your Child Testing You Or Being Manipulative?

No book can tell you when you need to stand firm or offer a softer touch, when your child's crying expresses weakness and manipulativeness that needs to be ignored or when it expresses real need that must be met. Only your clear, calm awareness can tell you this.

When your child demands something from you or reacts in a negative way to your disciplinary action, maintain your peace and poise. From that calm base, patiently pay attention to your child's behavior and to your inner feelings about it. If you notice anger, fear or guilt within yourself, do not let these feelings govern your action or speech. Letting them rule your behavior leads you to actions that generate further chaos and conflict with your child.

Sense intuitively what your child needs, and what you need, in the moment. You can only feel your intuition when your emotions settle into calmness and your mind settles into clarity. To achieve this state, try simply observing your emotions as they flow through you. By not reacting to your emotions, by simply letting them flow through you as you stay as relaxed as possible, they gradually pass.

Avoid hasty, emotional, impatient reactions. Unless real, immediate danger threatens, take time to calmly observe and consider the possibilities and your options before responding to your child's overbearing behavior.

Developing Your Disciplinary Strength And Skill

What if you agree with all this, but you still lack the self-discipline to take necessary disciplinary action? Simply start from where you are. Begin by exercising a little more self-control in an effort to maintain your peace and poise in response to your child's behavior. From there, start using the 1-2-3 Warning System and issue small consequences on which you can follow through easily. Making your child wait for an additional three minutes before allowing him to have the candy bar he wants as a consequence for whining may not seem strong enough, but it is a start.

Find the level of firmness to which you can hold consistently and build up gradually from there until you have the strength you need. If disciplining your child involves much struggle and strain on your part, you may be trying to take too much control. Your child only can change his behavior so fast, and you only can control so much at a time.

♦

27

Compassionate Discipline

Children understandably behave poorly in response to overly-harsh treatment they receive or to something that should be changed in their environment. For example, children who receive corporal punishment tend to exhibit more physically aggressive behavior toward others and toward themselves. While their hitting remains inexcusable, they have little choice but to behave toward others in a manner that others have behaved toward them. Young children forced to spend too much time in daycare may exhibit angry, overly aggressive behavior as well.

Making Positive Changes

You cannot always completely and perfectly meet your child's immediate needs. For instance, quitting your job to take your child out of daycare may be impossible. However, when you understand the contributing factors underlying your child's behavior, you can do something to help him. You can go to work on eliminating the problematic influences in your child's life and replace them with more of what he needs. Opportunity for some degree of positive change always exists. The child may need firm disciplinary action for his misbehavior, but he also needs -- and deserves -- to be provided with a situation that comes as close to honoring his true feelings and meeting his genuine needs as possible.

Avoiding Provocation

At any age, a child's overly-aggressive, defiant behavior or angry outbursts may occur as a reaction to numerous times when you have overlooked her sensitivities or unnecessarily thwarted or ignored her will. Be alert and recognize when you may be unconsciously overstepping your boundaries with your child, excessively imposing your will or ignoring her feelings.

For example, young children strongly dislike having someone clean their faces for them; they prefer cleaning their faces for themselves. Give your three year old a tissue and show him where to wipe. He will do a fine job and gain self-respect in the process. If you insist on forcing your child to tolerate constant imposition, he may respond with angry, aggressive, unhappy behavior that could have been avoided.

Understand, But Do Not Excuse Misbehavior

Provocation does not excuse anyone's improper actions, nor should it excuse your child's inappropriate behavior. To teach your child responsibility for her own actions, make her accountable for the way she behaves. If you do not do this, she learns to point to the flaws in others to justify her irresponsible responses. Take responsibility for the effect of your behavior upon your child, but also show your child that the way others behave toward her does not give her license to mistreat them.

For instance, if you do something that annoys your child, understand his annoyance, especially if you realize later that you really could have done things differently. However, if he reacts by shouting rudely at you, firmly inform him that this behavior is unacceptable. If he persists, issue a warning that a consequence will follow, or use the 1-2-3 Warning System.

Discuss The Problem

Later, have a calm discussion with your child (beginning at around age 4) during which you explain that you understand his frustration. You can apologize for what you did to provoke his behavior. Even if you provoked your child's misbehavior by doing something necessary, you should still sympathize with him for the fact that he found it unpleasant.

Then, explain what was inappropriate about the way your child behaved in reaction to your actions. Finally, help him discover more appropriate ways of communicating to you when he has a problem with your behavior toward him. Promise your child that you will listen to his complaints when he expresses them in a calm, respectful manner. Institute a new policy, such as a suggestion box or an appointment method.

"The Suggestion Box" And "The Appointment Method"

If your child is old enough to write, teach him to write down his complaints in a respectful statement, such as, "It bothers me when you tell me when to clean my room." Then, have a box into which he can drop the slip of paper. You promise to respond to his complaints within 48 hours. Within that time, make an appointment with him to calmly discuss the matter. This is called "The Suggestion Box Method."

When you make appointments without a suggestion box, you are using "The Appointment Method." It works like this: when your child has a problem with your behavior, she tells you she wants to make an appointment to discuss this matter. You either tell her when the two of you can meet, or you tell her that you will get back to her soon with a good time for the appointment. When you meet for your appointment, your child must speak to you in a calm, respectful manner. You agree to listen to her complaints about your treatment of her.

Responding To Your Child's Respectful Complaints

Respond to your child's respectful complaints with sensitivity and respect, not with defensiveness. Sincerely apologize for behaving toward her in a bothersome way, even when you see no alternative but to behave that way. Let her know you truly care about how she feels.

Next, discuss alternative options. For instance, if your child wants you to stop telling him when to clean his room, he needs to let you know when you can expect it to be cleaned. Children generally respond well to these kinds of compromises. When you show them respect and sensitivity for their feelings and interests you bring out their capacity for the same.

Compassionate Discipline

Disciplining with anger never works; disciplining with compassion does. Compassionate discipline is understanding and sympathizing with your child's feelings while maintaining the firmness your child needs to better direct his own behavior.

For instance, you can understand why your nine year old became angry at his little sister when she accidentally broke his model, but this does not excuse him from hitting her. Convey to him that you understand his reaction by saying, "I understand why you would feel angry about what your sister did after all the work you put into that model." Then, show him that her behavior does not excuse his behavior by saying, "However, hitting your sister is not allowed." If you feel it is appropriate, issue a consequence for his aggressive action.

If your child complains and says you seem less strict with his sister convey your compassionate understanding for his feelings. Do this by saying, "I can understand that you feel hurt and that you feel your sister deserves to be punished by us for what she did, but you have to trust in the way we raise her. How we parent each of you is our responsibility, not yours."

Teach Compassion

Avoid blaming your child for any tension, stress or frustration you feel when she behaves in ways you do not like. Take total responsibility for your own reactions to your child's actions, and strive every day to find easier, more effective and loving ways of relating with your child.

We teach children to behave responsibly as we practice taking responsibility for our own behavior and as we hold them accountable for their own behavior. We teach them to behave compassionately as we discipline ourselves to honor and serve them with love.

◆

28

Perfecting Your Disciplinary Skills

You can only exercise so much control over your child. Beyond that point it makes no sense to use more effort, because the additional effort depletes your energy and strains your nerves while accomplishing nothing. When you become exhausted from the constant frustration, stress and strain your experience with your child, you may assume that your child's behavior is to blame. However, your strain may be due to your own habitual over-reactions. It may seem that your child needs more discipline when, actually, you need to ease up on your child and on yourself.

The Energy Efficient Approach To Child Discipline

To avoid being excessive in *your* control tactics, pay close attention to your reactions to your child's actions. Recognize when you overreact or when you use more force or aggression than the situation warrants. Notice when you lose your composure, and take total responsibility for that. Strive to exert no excess effort or energy to accomplish your objectives with your child. Experiment with more loving, easier, gentler, relaxed, and natural ways of relating with your child until you find a way that expends the least amount of effort in the most pleasant and productive manner.

For example, do not speak more loudly or harshly than necessary. If it would be less of a strain to walk over to your child than to call him repeatedly from the other room, choose the easier way. Since your angry reactions only increase your child's anger toward you, replace your angry reactions with more loving responses. You can change any pattern of your behavior by small degrees at a time by simply paying closer attention, rather than reacting unconsciously and automatically, to them in the present moment.

This "energy-efficient" approach to child discipline helps you avoid unnecessarily arousing your child's oppositional defiance. When you use more force than necessary to achieve an objective, the excessive force you use ends up working against you -- often by showing up in your child's negative behavior.

The Gradient Scale Of Disciplinary Action

The energy efficient approach to child discipline requires applying as necessary a gradient scale of increasing degrees of firmness. Never apply more severity than necessary. Trust lenient loving kindness first.

Give your child responsibility for himself to the degree that seems reasonable to you, although children can usually do far more than we assume. Cautiously test your child's ability to function independently. When his behavior demonstrates a need for parental intervention, apply a bit more severity; choose a course of action involving a degree more sternness. Test him at that level, and progressively increase the force of your control by degrees and as needed.

Using this gradient scale of disciplinary action, the next time your child's behavior disturbs you, first tolerantly overlook his misbehavior; instead of reacting negatively, show him love, kindness, trust, encouragement, and respect for who he is, not what he did. Focus on his goodness and respond only to that. Feel and act as if you believe in him. If you feel any resentment or anger toward him, accept your negative emotional reaction as indicative of work you need to do on yourself, not on your child.

This purely positive way of relating to the child often discharges a child's anger and defensiveness, which may result in him quickly improving his behavior on his own. Your show of patience, love, tolerance, and trust inspires his trust, respect, appreciation, and cooperation.

Reasonable Discussions

Develop your ability to discuss things with your child. Make each attempt to discuss issues a practice and learning experience. Practice remaining calmer and more harmonious during discussions. Pay attention to what happens during the discussion. Such observation helps you learn to speak so your child really hears what you say and how to listen so you really hear what your child says.

Even three year olds have improved their behavior as a result of reasonable talks. Learn how to discuss subjects effectively with your child so you neither bore her nor turn her off to the discussion.

Firmly State The Rule

One disciplinary tack consists of informing your child of a rule in a sharp, firm manner -- without anger or stress but with stern seriousness. When your child behaves in a manner you want to discourage, go to her immediately and, while bending to her level, look directly into her eyes, and firmly state, "That is not allowed." You can offer her one brief statement that explains why you believe what you have said is true. For instance, if she just hit another child, kneel down to her level and sharply state: "Hitting is not allowed, because you must respect the other person's body" -- or "because it hurts" or "because people are not for hitting."

Following your sharp statement, either quickly guide your child into another activity in a positive and loving way, or simply return to your positive and loving way of relating with her. To regain a positive energy and communication flow between yourself and your child, use Building right away.

If your child continues to misbehave after you try this a few times, do not endlessly repeat this method or you run the risk of falling into a pattern of nagging or screaming. Move on to more aggressive disciplinary options that do not involve your negative behavior.

Your Disciplinary Options

In this book, I have described several basic disciplinary options. Let's review them now in order of increasing firmness. The number beside each option indicates its degree of firmness with number "1" indicating the least aggressive.

When you feel the need to become firmer than a firm statement of the rules, consider:

1.   Using **Conscious Detachment** - remove your attention from your child while she misbehaves, to teach her that poor behavior does not achieve the reward of making her the center of attention.

2.   Allowing the child to learn from **Natural Consequences** (the unpleasant consequences his behavior brings upon himself).

3.   Administering **Negative Consequences** using the **1-2-3 Warning and Consequence System**.

Basic Guidelines

The basic guidelines for effectively administering your disciplinary options include the following:

1.   *Maintain your peace and poise in response to your child's behavior.*

2.   *Consistently use the 1-2-3 Warning System before issuing a consequence.*

3.   *Consistently follow through on the consequences you issue.*

4.   ***Do not strain yourself or undermine your authority by arguing or using force.*** Do not use reasoning to force your child's compliance to make him understand your viewpoint or in an effort to save him from ignoring your rules and receiving a negative consequence.

5.   ***Use Building.*** Consistently demonstrate your unconditional love and acceptance of the child's true self.

6.   ***Have discussions.*** At another time, discuss with your child about why you needed to correct his behavior or impose a consequence and to hear his side of the issue.

Methods Alone Do Not Work

Sooner or later your child will outgrow any method or trick of child discipline you try. Only your authentic growth in love, wisdom and the intelligent application of your energy in the relationship will work consistently. As in any relationship, we cannot fool or manipulate our way to success with our children. We need to be willing ourselves to grow up and, in so doing, to relate more consciously with our children. This provides the only reliable way to bring about the best possible results in our relationship with them.

Achieving better results with your child requires nothing more and nothing less than your own continuing growth process. This is the key to parenting with love.

♦

◆

PART IV

PARENTING SOLUTIONS
And
LIVING, LOVING
RELATIONSHIP SOLUTIONS

◆

Introduction To Solutions #1 - 13

Parenting Solutions

The basic strategic guidelines that follow provide you with a framework on which to build your own unique and natural way of parenting with love in specific situations. Parenting methods provide no substitute for conscious alertness, emotional self-control and a willingness to grow. In other words, methods need to be applied skillfully to work. When applied skillfully, many parents have found the methods that follow to be extremely helpful.

The Key Loving Ingredient

Simply applying a child discipline method may not address the real problem, the problem that lies at the root of your child's misbehavior. At any given moment, your child's disturbing behavior results from a synthesis of all of the factors affecting his life up to that moment, including the way *you* behave. The child who resists going to bed, for example, may be expressing his legitimate need for more attention, more physical exercise during the day, more order in his schedule, more time with you, more stability in his home life, more tolerance from a parent, more consistent firmness from a parent, or more time to prepare for bedtime. The child who behaves poorly does not necessarily demonstrate a discipline problem but rather a natural, honest reaction to his .

Never relate to your child as a "bother." The instant you do, that is what your child becomes. Your child will respond best when she feels truly loved, cared about and appreciated.

Practice

You may learn the finest methods for achieving your child's compliance, yet, because of your own lack of self-discipline still not apply them. In this book you have been presented with practices you can begin using right now to build the perception and inner strength you need to know what is truly right to do and actually to do it. These practices include Conscious Parenting and maintaining your peace and poise. If you exercise these two practices alone to whatever degree possible you develop the perception and the power of self-discipline to parent with love more effectively everyday.

If you find yourself unable to institute the basic parenting solutions that follow, go back to the earlier sections of this book and continue working on the practices and understanding described there.

The sections that follow present sample strategies for dealing with some of the typical challenges parents face daily. See them as general pointers rather than as hard and fast rules.

◆

Solution #1

Ending Bedtime Battles

If your child's bedtime tends to be difficult, maintain your peace and poise no matter what happens. Do not permit *yourself* to use anger, arguing, pleading, nagging, shouting, or spanking to control the situation. Losing your peace and poise increases the stimulation offered to your child, and at bedtime you want to increase the calm in the home. Even if your child defies or ignores you and begins acting out aggressively when you say it is time for bed, concentrate on not reacting with anger or stress.

By degrees, bring more peace and order into the situation by looking for small ways to make the bedtime process flow more smoothly and easily and by withdrawing your energy by degrees from the battles.

For Children Two Through Twelve Years Of Age

Here are some strategies for getting your child into bed on time and with as little conflict as possible:

1. ***Begin bedtime preparations one hour before the bedtime ritual.*** Since children generally have difficulty making sudden transitions, keep the general home environment peaceful and harmonious as bedtime approaches. Begin preparing your child and your home for bedtime at least one hour in advance of her bedtime. Wind down the pace and intensity of activities. Soften the lighting. Function more quietly. Do not have intense music or television shows playing. Exhibit relaxation and

peace in your behavior. Do not engage in intense discussions with your child or with your spouse. In your mind, begin thinking about and envisioning how you want your child's bedtime to proceed. You might also plant seeds in your child's mind about the approach of bedtime; every five or 10 minutes, mention that bedtime is approaching. Do this in a pleasant, positive manner, not as a warning or a threat.

2. ***Institute a bedtime ritual.*** The more regularity you bring into your child's bedtime procedure, the more smoothly it will flow. Set a time when your child begins preparing for bed, and leave your child's room at the same time every night. (This means you cannot lie down with your child if you tend to fall asleep with him, otherwise he will come to depend upon you doing so.) Make every aspect of bedtime a nightly ritual with clear and distinct steps leading up to sleep, and withdraw yourself from the process gradually. When circumstances make it impossible to stick to the regular bedtime, at least stick to the regular routine or ritual. To the best of your ability, begin this routine every night at the same time.

3. ***Withdraw yourself from the process.*** As soon as possible, begin withdrawing yourself from each stage of your child's bedtime preparation. Do this gradually in small, unnoticeable degrees at first. You might begin by having your child turn the faucets for handwashing. Then, have her wash her own hands, but you still dry them. Then, have her dry them, but you hang up the towel. Then, she does all of her own washing and hangs up the towel as you observe. Then, she does it on her own, and you come into the bathroom when she finishes to inspect the bathroom and see that she is clean. Praise her for every step she handles on her own. If she does something poorly, do not be critical. Preparations for bedtime need to be kind, non-stressful and easy going.

4. *When your child handles bedtime preparations by himself, have him come to you or call for you when he is ready for bed.* Check to see if all his bedtime preparations have been done well. Do not be strict in your reaction, or you may incite rebellion or over-stimulate him. If his preparations have all been completed to your satisfaction, go to his room and complete the nightly ritual, such as reading stories before kissing him goodnight.

5. *Use less time spent with you as the logical consequence to bedtime tardiness.* Establish the routine that your child is to begin preparing for bed (washing and putting on pajamas) 30 minutes before you leave her room for the night. If she dawdles over or resists doing her bedtime preparations, do not argue or nag. Simply warn her that the more time she takes getting ready, the less time she will have with you when her preparations are complete. Do not repeat this more than twice. The longer it takes her to ready herself for bed, the less story time she has with you. This represents a logical consequence, since you do not read until her preparations are completed and you leave her room at the same time each night.

6. *If your child cries out for you after you leave his room, delay your response.* Before your child goes to bed, make sure he has his cup of water on the night stand and that everything in his room is adjusted just the way he likes it for sleep. If he cries out for you after you leave, delay your response. Give him the opportunity to learn how to settle himself down. If he persists, go to him slowly and calmly. Children often call parents to their room one time to make sure they will respond if an emergency were to occur. Do not engage in much conversation. Respond to what he has to say, and then tell him that he needs to go to sleep now and that you will see him in the morning.

7. ***If your child cries for you again and again after being put to bed, do not react with a show of emotion or impatience.*** Consider the facts of the situation, the possibilities and your options before choosing your response. Does she really need more contact with you? Is she just wound-up and needs to settle herself down? When you lack certainty, choose a moderate option avoiding extremes. You may lengthen the time you stay away or shorten the time you stay with her. You might return just once to give her some reassuring words.

8. ***If your child leaves his room, remain calm.*** If he leaves his room to go to the bathroom on his own once, or even twice, ignore that. If he wanders out to see what you are doing, remain calm and cool. You can give him a hug or a moment of loving attention, but then inform him that he needs to go back to bed and to stay there. If he leaves his room again, warn him that the next time he leaves the door will be closed for a specified period (one minute per year of life). If he leaves after that, follow through. If he leaves again, warn him that next time he does so the door will be locked for the same period of time. If your child's door normally is closed and he leaves, warn him that the door will be locked for a specific amount of time (one minute per year of life) if he leaves again. When the time is up, unlock the door. If he leaves after this, repeat this procedure.

Note: Regard your child's bedtime behavior as a symptom of her daytime experience. If she routinely exhibits non-compliant behavior at bedtime, you may need to make changes in the way you relate to her during the day. Think about what she needs more of to be happy, cooperative or self-disciplined, and begin making small changes that help fill her daytime needs. For instance, she simply may need more quality time with you. If you then look more carefully at your options, you will see at least some way that you can better meet this need, thus turning your child's bedtime into a smoothly-flowing, stress-free routine.

For Children Older Than Twelve

At some point, you will have to leave bedtime up to your child. You can still establish rules about when your child needs to be in his room up to about the age of 16. As he stays in his room and does not disturb anyone, give him the responsibility of determining how much sleep he needs. If you go to bed first, you can allow him to stay out of his room if he chooses. Again, he must not keep others awake.

If your child stays up so late that he tends to oversleep in the morning, refer to "Solution # 3: Leaving On Time In The Morning."

If your teen persists in creating a disturbance at night when others need peace and quiet for sleep, this may indicate a problem ineffectively handled by simple child discipline alone. Such behavior indicates that your child feels angry about something that she takes quite seriously.

Have discussions with her separate from her bedtime routine. Try to discover what troubles her by demonstrating a willingness to address *her* issues.

◆

Solution #2

Nighttime Crying And Having The Child Sleep In Her Own Bed

While all babies, especially those younger than six months of age, wake in the night and cry either for food or for the comfort of their parents, some children have trouble sleeping through the night even when they are much older. Parents of such children often suffer from low energy caused by their lack of or interrupted nighttime sleep, which, in turn, affects their ability to parent effectively during the day. Children also feel the affects of lessened or interrupted nighttime sleep in their own behavior during the day. Therefore, finding a solution to this problem is important to all involved.

The First 30 Months of Life

During the first two or two and a half years of life, your child may want to sleep with you, rather than in her crib, as much as possible.   However, no universal law delineates whether allowing her to sleep with you is right or wrong. Ultimately, the judgment is yours, and whether she sleeps with you or not remains your decision. If you would prefer that she sleep in her own bed throughout the night, though, you will want to avoid creating her habit of sleeping with you at as young an age as possible.

Two Considerations

Make your decision about sharing a bed with your child based on two factors. First, consider what you honestly feel is best for your child's progress toward healthy self-reliance. Second, consider what is in the best interest of your marriage. Bringing your child to bed may remove the privacy and romance you and your spouse need to keep your marriage rich in intimacy and passion. Remember that your child ultimately benefits when you and your spouse feel the deep, romantic bonding that strengthens your marriage.

The Ideal Bed

During your child's first year of life, you actually might find that you are better off with the infant in the same room, not necessarily in the same bed, as you. This way, she can be close to you without actually being in your bed, and this arrangement may prevent her from developing the habit of sleeping with you in the first place (some studies indicate that the infant benefits from hearing the breathing patterns of the parents in the night, this can diminish the risk of Sudden Infant Death Syndrome). If you do not place your infant in a crib but instead give her a low mattress on the ground she may not want to sleep with you as much or at all. The crib that protects a child from a bad fall also separates and contains her. The ideal bed for a baby consists of something she can leave and enter as she pleases without hurting herself. However, only place such a bed in an environment that provides her with child-proofed freedom.

Your Psychological Preparation

Many parenting challenges offer no easy or painless resolutions, but you can learn how to improve your peace, poise and patience and to maintain a more positive and loving attitude to make these trying times less difficult. Infant night crying presents this kind of challenge, and it would be best for all parents to be psychologically and situationally prepared for the event.

Many infants cry in the night until their mother lifts them up and holds them. This is especially true of newborns. They fall asleep in mamma's loving embrace, but the moment they find themselves back in the crib their crying may start up again. Of course, babies wake in the night repeatedly crying to be fed or changed. Some young children just cry out for mother in the night to be sure they are not alone. This is a normal stage in any child's life, and many experts agree that a very young infant cannot be spoiled by being picked up and held as often as they cry for such contact.

Psychological preparations for infant night crying involves accepting the likelihood of your infant's night crying. If you know that sleep deprivation is part of the parenting experience, you can be more understanding, flexible and patient when it occurs.

If you cannot sleep through the night, at least give yourself all the rest possible. The more relaxed you feel, the more rest you receive. Becoming tense or impatient drains you of more energy. Breathe deeply and gently while awake with your child. Remain as pleasant and peaceful as possible. Trust that you can get through this, and do not permit yourself to worry about how you will feel in the morning.

Situational Preparation

Effective parenting, especially during the first three years of your child's life, is a day- and night-time job. However, you need a certain amount of sleep to function. Your child may not allow you to get enough sleep at night, especially in the first four or five months after birth.

If you did not, or could not, prepare your life to accommodate the night demands of the parenting task, then you have placed yourself at a disadvantage. To compensate for your lack of sleep at night, you must function in low-gear during much of the following day. Make conservation of your energy priority number one. If you have to work at a full-time job, you will not have the energy to stress yourself out over anything. Practice self-maintenance constantly. Watch your eating. Give yourself the healthy physical exercise you need. Take five minute breaks whenever you can during which you sit still, breathe deeply and relax fully.

Minimizing Your Infant's Night Crying

Remember that in the first 6 months of your child's life, her nighttime cries may seem unnecessary (she was just fed, has no gastrointestinal discomfort, has a clean and dry diaper), but she may have a legitimate need for contact or the security of knowing someone is nearby. You must decide, based on your knowledge of your child, when she is old enough or emotionally ready to begin the process of eliminating her night crying. Surely, the first two or three months of her life are too early.

To eliminate nighttime crying, increase the amount of time before you respond to your child by small degrees each night. As you do so, you will get a feel for how long you can stay away. Learning the best reaction time for your child represents a sensitive task. React too slowly and your child learns that no one responds when she needs attention; react too quickly and your child does not learn to pacify or calm herself.

After the age of 18 months, occasional nights in bed with you are harmless as long as they do not become a habit. However, even when he is permitted to sleep with you, make it your business to wake him and either send or escort him back to his own bed before the night is through.

If you need to establish firmly for your child a pattern of spending the night in his own bed, try the following:

1. *If your child comes into your room crying and asks to sleep with you, tell him that he needs to sleep in his own bed and send him back to his room.*

2. ***If your child does not return to his room on his own, escort him.*** Do not permit any talking, show no emotion and keep all lights low to avoid stimulating him. Give him an opportunity to use the bathroom before returning to bed.

3. ***If your child says he feels too frightened to be alone in his room, sit in a chair beside his bed.*** Tell him you will stay with him for a few minutes while he goes back to sleep. Warn him that if he cries or talks, you will leave. If he starts crying or talking, start counting using the 1-2-3 Warning System and time yourself out of his room if you reach three. If you reach three, leave. Do not lie down in bed with your child; if you do, you might as well let him sleep with you.

4. ***Remain sitting beside your child's bed for a few minutes, then leave.*** If he cries out after you leave him alone, ignore him for as long as possible. This gives him the chance to settle down on his own. Discipline yourself to stay away for a little longer than feels comfortable. This teaches your child that he cannot control you by crying, and it breaks your habit of automatically reacting to his tears or demands.

5. ***If your child's crying continues to the point that you feel you have to go to him again, repeat the chair routine.***

6. ***Repeat this procedure for as long as necessary until your child accepts the new pattern.*** If you have perpetuated your child's habit of sleeping with you whenever he wakes or cries in the night this may go on for several nights, but it will eventually work.

7. *If your child sneaks into your bed without waking you, or sneaks into your room to sleep on the floor beside you, inform him firmly the next day that this demonstrates a disrespect for your privacy.* If you wake up and find him there, wake him and send him to his room, escorting him if he refuses to go on his own. If this happens again, warn your child that the next time he does this he will receive a consequence. If it happens a third time, follow through by restricting one of his privileges the following day.

8. *If your child shares his room with a sibling, and his night crying wakes your other child, you have a logistical problem.* Because your child knows you do not want his cries to disturb his sibling's sleep, crying may be his way of forcing you to allow him to sleep in your bed. You do not have to be controlled by this. One solution may be to move the sleeping child out of the room while the other carries on.

◆

Solution #3

Leaving On Time In The Morning

The more you feel pressured to leave your home on time in the morning, the more uncooperativeness your child may demonstrate. Children under the age of six especially resist fitting into their parent's schedule, because the schedule itself and your demand that it be met makes them feel left out, unimportant and dominated.

To achieve your child's smooth cooperation in the morning, or at other times, create situations in which his genuine needs are met, and his genuine limitations are honored. Try giving your child five or 10 minutes of your totally focused, intimate attention and loving involvement before he has to get ready to leave the house and before you focus on preparing yourself to leave. This may meet your child's genuine need to feel significant, valued and respected, which teaches him to cooperate willingly with you and to treat your needs as important.

Children behave better when freed from the burden of time pressure. We usually regard our hurry as necessary. However, it actually is much more necessary to eliminate the hurry from your life. Rush brings out the worst in all of us, including our children. Constant hurry in your life is self-imposed, avoidable and destructive.

As mentioned earlier, the child-discipline problem you think you have in the morning actually may be your own time-management problem. If your child's slow pace causes you stress, take time to re-design your morning schedule. You may have to go to bed earlier yourself to enable yourself to wake up earlier, thus giving you more time to move through the stages of morning preparation in a calm, natural and relaxed pace.

Adjusting your morning schedule may not be the answer. Your child may need more structure. The following guidelines have helped parents achieve this.

For Children Ages Two Through Twelve Years

1. *Establish a set morning routine and stick to it consistently every workday morning.*

2. *As early as possible begin teaching your child the exact steps you want her to follow in preparation for leaving in the morning.* From the age of two, begin teaching your child how to prepare herself on her own to leave. If your child is three or four years old, give her an alarm clock and show her how to use it. Show her how to wash and dress herself, clean her room, make her bed, and prepare and eat her own breakfast.

3. *Watch your expectations.* You may realize that you expect your child to go through the morning routine like a well-oiled machine rather than as a natural child. Adjust your schedule to accommodate your child's natural, unforced pacing. Discover a reasonable pace to expect from him. Children adopt the behavior patterns around them *that are within their capacity.* Do not expect your child to race through his morning preparations with your level of skill.

4. *Gradually turn the responsibilities of getting ready over to your child.* Sometimes all a child needs is for her parents to allow her to do what she need to do. Children rebel when they feel overly bossed. Try staying out of the process when your child is physically capable of handling her own morning preparations (by the age of 3 years old). Trust and expect the child to succeed. Resist the urge to prod or warn her when she seems to be running late.

5. *If your child runs late and does not have time to eat, let missing breakfast be the natural consequence for dawdling.*

6. *Do not nag, plead or exhibit anger or stress if your child runs late.* Convey to your child the message that all responsibility for being ready on time belongs to him. If he needs your help with any task, offer your assistance once or twice. If he resists, walk away and focus on your own preparations.

7. *If your child runs too late, she leaves as she is.* If your child has not changed out of her pajamas by the time you have to leave, stuff a paper bag with some clothes and take her to the car. She can get dressed quickly in the back seat if she chooses. Project the attitude that if your child wants to go to school in her pajamas or half-dressed, it is her choice. Most children do not want to make this choice even once. After that, your child will promptly fulfill her responsibilities in the morning.

8. *For children aged six through the teen years, use consequences when necessary.* If your child's morning delay tactics become a pattern, start using privilege restrictions as the consequence for morning irresponsibility.

9. *An appropriate consequence for oversleeping is enforcement of an earlier bedtime.*

10. **For teens, if the problem persists, a more serious conflict may exist between you and your child.** Review the principles and practices in this book, and pay more attention to determining what is really bothering your child.

◆

Solution #4

Discouraging Disturbing Control Tactics

The next time you need help dealing with a typical disturbing control tactic, such as nagging, whining, bossiness, screaming, disrespectfulness, tantrums, arguing, and hitting, review the following pointers and use them to rechannel your child's energy.

1. *Do not permit yourself to be controlled or manipulated by your child's tactics.* If you allow your child to control you with this type of behavior, you teach her that disturbing others works; thus, she will use it again. When your child's negative behavior triggers a negative emotional reaction in you or makes you give in to her demands, she takes control from you. Work on strengthening your self-control when your child uses poor behavior to control you.

2. *Avoid demonstrating these tactics yourself.* For example, do not nag your child to do what *you* want or whine or scream when *he* does not comply. The behavior you exhibit teaches your child to behave in exactly the same way.

3. *When your child persists in using these tactics even after you direct her to stop, use the 1-2-3 Warning System followed by a consequence.* When children behave in any of these ways, many parents find that a Time Out or withholding whatever the child is using the control tactic to obtain works well as a consequence to reaching the

count of three. For instance, if he is whining for a cookie, you could say, "That's one. If I reach three there will not only be no cookie now but no cookie later as well."

4. ***If your child becomes caught up in a tantrum, do not use reason to control her.*** Raising your voice for any reason runs the risk of escalating tensions. A raised voice raises your stress level and makes it easier for you to lose your self-control and overreact before you realize yourself even doing so. Time Out works well with tantrums. Another Time Out option parents have used for tantrums involves leaving the room themselves. In other words, the parent leaves the child alone until he calms down. Simply picking the child up and placing him in his room for his Time Out also works well.

In any event, show your child that her tantrum does not dominate you. At a later time, show her how to throw a "good" tantrum to release her frustrations. She can go to her room and punch her mattress, for example. If she needs to scream, show her how to muffle the sound in her pillow. Do not teach her that anger is wrong; teach her to express this emotion harmlessly. If tantrums become a pattern for your child, it means she has found that they work. In other words, she either gets you to give in or she gets you upset when she throws a tantrum. At a time when you both are calm, say to her, "An automatic rule applies to your tantrums: Whatever you throw a tantrum for you cannot have. If you do not scream or cry when telling me you want something, I will always be willing to listen to you and consider your requests." If a time out consequence produces unsatisfactory results, try other privilege restrictions instead of or in addition to.

◆

Solution #5

Improving Mealtime Behavior

Follow the same routine and rituals at every mealtime (especially dinnertime), and your child will have an easier time behaving in an orderly, well-mannered fashion during the meal. Let dinner be at the same time and at the same place with the same people every evening. You can create variety by making every Tuesday evening, for example, eat-out night and every Sunday a special family dinner. In other words, make the variety a stable pattern as well.

Establish Boundaries

Be clear about what you expect during mealtime, and do not use nagging, pleading, complaining or criticizing achieve this. Inform your child clearly at times other than mealtime of the table manners you require of him.

Require your child to remain seated at the table throughout the meal, unless he needs to leave the table for a good reason. If your young one wants out of his highchair, try moving it closer to the table or making other adjustments. If that does not work, let him try sitting on telephone books on a regular chair to let him feel more grown up (beginning at age two). Tell him that sitting this way represents a privilege that he loses if he does not remain in his seat. If the meal drags on longer than normal, let him leave at his normal time. Permit teens to leave the table early if they choose, but if you keep the mealtime pleasant they will want to stay longer.

Keep the following guidelines in mind as you formulate your approach to mealtime behavior:

1. ***Demonstrate what you want to teach.*** Consistently demonstrate the mealtime behavior you want her to exhibit as she matures. Remain calm and relaxed while dining in your child's presence. Speak politely, softly and slowly while being careful to maintain a pleasant, tranquil eating atmosphere at all times. Eat consciously, with attention focused on eating, but not so focused on your food that you lose touch with the social aspects of the meal. Based on The Law of Reflection, children automatically adopt the behavior patterns to which they consistently are exposed.

2. ***Remain non-reactive when your child behaves in a disturbing manner.*** When your child exhibits poor table manners or behaves in a disturbing manner at the table, do not permit yourself to react with anger, stress or criticism. In other words, remain non-reactive. When you react with a strong show of annoyance, you increase the general air of tension, and the negative attention you direct at your child teaches him he can dominate the situation and command all the attention he wants by behaving improperly. The practice of non-reactivity, or Conscious Detachment, means that you give your child *less* attention and *no* power to make you react with anger or stress when he behaves inappropriately. (This does not mean that you take no steps toward correcting his behavior.)

3. ***Provide your child with a sense of belonging.*** When your child feels like a significant part of the mealtime gathering, she loses the need to misbehave as a means of standing out. Pay attention to her when she is <u>not</u> misbehaving. Demonstrate interest in her by asking her questions and listening to her answers. Ask follow-up questions to stimulate her thinking. Do not just ask, "How was your day?" Ask what the teacher wore and how you

child felt about it. Inquire as to why she felt that way. Exploring the details of her experience with her helps to her feel important.

4. ***If your child's behavior becomes too disturbing to overlook, use the 1-2-3 Warning System.*** The logical consequence for you reaching three is a Time Out away from the table. If that means your child does not get to finish his meal, refer to #8 below.

5. ***Avoid conflicts over your menu by telling your child in advance what she will be eating.*** If your child wants to construct a weekly menu with you, be willing to do that. Tell your child what you want to make for dinner. If she does not want that, give her one or two other options that provide her with a reasonably-balanced, healthy meal that you agree to prepare. If she chooses to eat the same thing every night, do not resist much -- as long as preparing that meal does not feel too inconvenient for you and the foods meet her basic nutritional needs.

6. ***If you prepare the meal for which your child asked but he decides not eat it, do not make this into a conflict of wills.*** Simply inform your child that you will not prepare any more food for him tonight. If he wants to fix himself something to eat, and he can do so without your assistance, there is no good reason not to permit that. However, if rejecting what he requested becomes a pattern, he loses the option of choosing what you cook for him.

7. ***Do not attempt to force your child to eat, to take another bite or to finish what is on her plate.*** The compulsion to have your child finish all the food on her plate develops patterns of compulsive eating that can lead to weight problems later. Thin people do *not* feel the need to finish what is on their plate, and they do *not* eat past the point of feeling full.

8. ***If your child does not finish what is on his plate, he
   forfeits desert and you refuse to prepare food for him
   later.*** Be sure to give your child small portions to make
   success easy. If he fails to finish and feels hungry later,
   however, he can snack on dinner's left-overs or prepare
   himself a sandwich on his own without your assistance.
   Demonstrate respect for yourself and establish the structure
   he needs by ending your kitchen duties with the conclusion
   of dinner.

9. ***Permit your child to prepare his own meals or to help
   in their preparation.*** This gives children a feeling of
   healthy contribution and importance.   Children often
   demonstrate better table manners and eating patterns when
   they feel a sense of contribution to the meal. Even having
   the youngest child help with setting the table, or setting his
   own plate, can result in desirable mealtime behavior.

Restaurants

Eating with children in restaurants can feel like an
extremely trying, rather than a pleasurable, event. If your child
quickly becomes impatient in restaurants, take some kind of
game with you that he can play while waiting for service. You
might even bring him a bag of cold vegetables to munch on
while he waits.

During the meal, if your child acts out, calmly but
firmly use the 1-2-3 Warning System, with the consequence
being a Time Out away from the table. (You probably will
have to leave with him and stay by him during the Time Out.)
Another warning you can try is, "If I reach three, we will not
order pizza at home this week."

If your child consistently behaves poorly in restaurants,
stop taking him until he matures enough to handle this
experience in an appropriate manner. You can tell your child
that this may be the consequence for continued inappropriate
restaurant behavior.

For Children With Special Needs

If your child has a health problem, such as diabetes, mealtime may present a more serious issue. Eliminating your emotional reactions to your child's unwillingness to eat properly becomes far more difficult -- but more crucial than ever -- under these circumstances. If you become emotional when your child resists eating, she may use resistance as a way of taking out her frustration on you.

Do not nag, plead or argue to get your child to eat, and do not offer rewards for eating. Allow children over the age six to be responsible for themselves. By allowing your child to make herself ill by not meeting her own eating needs, she will learn from natural consequences to be more responsible and less dependent upon you to rescue her. (Before doing this, check with your doctor to find out how far you can let the situation go before you must step in and take over.)

When the time comes to step in, issue consequences for your child's non-cooperation. Do not baby or coddle your child or you teach her that she can receive more assistance and concern from people through uncooperativeness and irresponsibility. If she resists when she really must eat something, force feed her without emotion. Later, have discussions with her to help her understand her situation and to feel good about herself as she is.

◆

Solution #6

Handling Phone Interruptions

Parents needs to develop the skill of *not* reacting with annoyance to their child's interruptions, otherwise they doom themselves to these painful feelings on a regular basis -- in fact, whenever they use the telephone. When you respond with peace and poise, rather than frustration, to distractions from and interruptions to your phone conversations. You create a happier, more positive, more mutually-respectful relationship with your child. At the same time, you strengthen your flexibility, making it possible for you to easily and competently shift your focus without feeling stressed.

Begin by taking responsibility for the way in which you react to telephone interruptions. Work on controlling your reaction to the interruption rather than on controlling the child who does the interrupting. With practice and alert awareness, you can change your habit of automatically reacting with anger and frustration when your focus of attention has to shift from the phone conversation to your child.

The more frustrated, impatient or overwhelmed you feel when your child tries to interfere with your phone call, the more stressful and chaotic the situation becomes. The first step to gaining effective control of the situation is to not allow the situation to control your emotional reaction. Just maintaining your calm and patience can be enough to keep things peacefully progressing in a positive direction.

The 1-2-3 Warning System

When you want to institute more structure or control over the situation, use the 1-2-3 Warning System. If you have used this system consistently for other situations, it will work well in this one also.

When your child asks or acts out for your attention while you are on the phone, firmly but politely ask her to wait until your phone conversation ends. If she ignores this request, hold up a finger and firmly state, "That's one. If I reach three, you have a consequence." If you already know the consequence, you can tell your child what it will be.

For many parents, the Time Out consequence has proven effective in this situation. If you use Time Out, send the child to his Time Out place if you reach three.

Teach Courtesy

Avoid being too strict about your child's interruptions during your phone conversations. Develop the patience and flexibility to give your child some attention and love while you are on the phone. Seek easy and gentle ways of soothing the child for the duration of the phone call. In addition, teach your child the polite and courteous way to interrupt a phone call. By providing him with access to you through well-mannered behavior, he feels less need to use ill-mannered behavior for control.

◆

Solution #7

Achieving Room-Cleaning Compliance

Struggling to force your child to keep his room as tidy as you would like may be more trouble than it is worth. Remember, trying to control your child in any situation expends your energy. Do not be so attached to having your way in minor things that you neglect to clearly consider the amount of energy you must expend to win.

You may accomplish more by staying out of this particular matter. Every time you make a decision for your child, he loses the opportunity, and perhaps the motivation, to make responsible decisions for himself. As a result of assuming the role of director and decision-maker in his life, you may think of him as constantly needing your direction. In response, he may fail to develop the ability he needs to make responsible decisions for himself.

Giving your child responsibility for himself in the area of cleaning his room helps him feel more grown up. This actually can result in more mature and responsible behavior in general, even if his room remains messy. Your child may appreciate you letting him be his own boss on this issue, and that can translate into more cooperative and loving behavior from him in more important areas.

Finally, when you allow your child to live in the messy room he creates for himself, you allow him to learn from the natural consequences of a disorderly environment. You might believe that he likes the mess or, at least, that he does not mind it. Give him the chance to experience it for a while without saying anything. If you involve yourself, he may keep it messy on purpose either to annoy you or to rebel against your over-involvement. If you let him decide when or if to clean his room, he may find the natural consequences unsettling enough to begin cleaning his room on his own.

To implement more structure, consider the following:

1. ***During your child's first six years of life you have the opportunity to develop her motivation and self-discipline in the area of cleanliness.*** Prior to the age of six, children are sensitive to order and extremely open to learning to maintain it. They want to do what they see being done around them.

   - **During your child's first year**, keep her near you and let her watch you as you clean and neaten various areas of your home. You may want to explain what you are doing. Think of your words and actions as seeds you plant in her subconscious that will bear the fruit of her similar abilities or tendencies later.

   - **At around the age of one**, give your child tiny cleaning tasks that she accomplishes with your help. For instance, after she sees you picking something up from the floor and placing it where it belongs, guide her through a similar process. Guide her hand to pick something up, and help her to hold it as you lead her to the place it belongs. Then, help her to put the object down carefully in its place.

   - **At around the age of two**, give your child whatever cleaning tasks she can handle. You can stay with her as company or as her helper.

   - **By the age of three**, if you have followed the previous steps, you need not be anything but your child's coach as she does the entire job of cleaning her room on her own.

   - **By the time your child reaches six**, she will have a strong sensitivity to order that will motivate her toward neatness, and she will have built the habit of cleaning her room on her own.

2. *If your child is older than six and in the habit of keeping a messy room, let the natural consequences of the disorder motivate him to take better charge of his environment.* Make his room his responsibility. If the mess bothers you, close the door to his room and do not look inside.

3. *When you can stand it no longer, ask your child to clean her room.* If she resists, give her the choice of doing what you ask or receiving a consequence.

4. *If the consequence for not cleaning his room has no effect, consider additional consequences.* If your child willingly sacrifices all of his privileges to keep his room a mess, let him do so. Living on restricted privileges will develop his self-discipline. However, things rarely go this far. If your child resists cleaning his room this strongly, his behavior signals a need for more understanding. Talk with him. Work on building up your positive, loving rapport. Show him that you care about whatever may be bothering him, and demonstrate your willingness to help him with his problems.

5. *For better compliance, make room cleaning a prerequisite for something your child wants to do or wants you to do for her.* This approach falls into the category of Pre-Arranged Consequences. Do not wait until you want her to clean her room to implement this consequence, though. Have a discussion with your child in which you clearly define the room-cleaning schedule you require of her and the privileges she preserves by maintaining that schedule. When she forgets, do not remind her. On the day that she was to have her room cleaned, administer the consequence for non-compliance.

6. ***Establish a weekly schedule.*** It will probably take too much energy to get your child to clean his room every day, especially if he did not go through the preparations for this in his first six years of life. A weekly or bi-weekly schedule can work much better.

7. ***Use Building.*** Although you probably expect your child to keep her room clean, do not take her efforts in this area for granted. Notice when she makes any effort at all in this direction, and respond with praise. If she feels that you appreciate what she does, she will feel the desire to do more.

8. ***Definitely avoid negative emotional reactions, criticism or put-downs about your child's lack of room-cleaning compliance.*** Children need to feel more valued than their behavior. Becoming angry or critical when your child does not clean his room hurts his feelings and incites a rebellious response. Critical remarks, like calling your child "lazy" or "a slob," even said playfully, foster an irresponsible self-image, which reinforces the behavior you want to change.

The Playful Approach

Making your child's chores fun provides an easy, positive way to get compliance that enhances the loving feelings between you and your child. Turn room cleaning into a playful contest in which your child strives to outdo herself. You can call the game, "Room Cleaning Olympics," and use a stop watch to encourage her to beat her best room-cleaning time. Cheer her efforts and, after she has completed her chore, the two of you can sit down over a cool drink and talk about what a wonderful job she did.

Working With Teens

As children near the teen years they begin resenting being told how to manage their rooms. Therefore, remain as uninvolved as you can regarding this issue. It is too late to recreate your child's basic patterns and tendencies. The sloppiest teens often become the neatest adults, especially if they were surrounded by neatness and order in their first six years of life. If you clean your teen's room from time to time for him, no harm will be done, since his basic behavioral patterns are already formed.

If you have been using an approach similar to the one described in the above eight pointers, your teen probably will continue the pattern of cleaning his room on a weekly basis. When you want him to clean his room, ask him nicely, as a favor to you, and be careful not to make him feel like you are being bossy or treating him like a baby. An extremely sensitive, mature, adult approach generally works best with teens.

♦

Solution #8

Solving School Behavior Problems

Whether your child attends preschool or high school, do not wait for problems that occur at school to build until it becomes necessary for your child's teacher to call you. Teachers may wait to call parents until the problem has gotten too large for them to handle alone. By then, your child may be in too much trouble to change things quickly.

Start With The Positive

To prevent this situation from occurring, call your child's teacher every couple of weeks for a progress report. If the teacher says everything is fine, ask more specific questions.

Make your first specific questions positive ones, such as: "Can you tell me anything my child is doing right or well?" "Where has my child shown any degree of improvement?" "In what areas does he demonstrate any degree of excellence?" Asking positive questions helps your child's teacher recognize and appreciate your child's successes. You can help a teacher's relationship with your child by telling your child about the positive things the teacher had to say.

Problem Solving

After spending a few moments asking your child's teacher to offer a positive progress report, probe for signs of any developing problems. Ask the teacher to tell you about any difficulties she has with your child. However, make it clear that you are her teammate and that both of you are working *for* your child. Begin by asking the teacher, "Is there any way my child behaves that you find problematic to any degree?"

If behavior problems do exist, ask your child's teacher for a specific description of the disturbing behavior and, for each behavior problem, ask, "What approach are you taking to solve this problem?"

After the teacher answers this question, ask, "How is your method working for you?" When the teacher tells you the results, ask, "Is there anything you feel I can do at home to help my child do better in this area?"

Learn About Your Child

Whether the teacher has a problem with your child's behavior or not, you can learn from the teacher's experience with your child. Ask the teacher questions like: "What way of relating with my child do you find brings out his best?" or "Is there anything you feel I can do at home with my child to help him perform better at school or in life?"

Contribute to the teacher's understanding of your child by relating what you have tried that has or has not worked well for you in your relationship with your child. Share some of the things you have learned about how to deal with your child to achieve positive results. For instance, you may have found that your child responds better to gentle explanations of what is expected of her than harsh, firm, threatening demands for compliance.

Regularly discussing your child with his teacher in this way leads the teacher to give your child more than attention. Your questions prompt the teacher to think about and to observe your child more closely, and your combined experiences with your child help both of you best serve your child.

Do Not Turn The Teacher Into A "Snitch"

Avoid having these parent/teacher discussions in front of your child, unless you know your child will hear her teacher's praise rather than criticism. If your child hears her teacher complaining to you about her behavior, she may regard the teacher as a "snitch" and feel threatened and resentful. Discuss your child's progress with her teacher in private. If you discuss these matters over the phone, have the conversation at a time when your child is not around.

Inform your child that you are in contact with her teacher, but be careful about how you refer to her teacher's role. Do not portray the teacher as your spy. Describe your relationship with the teacher in positive terms. For instance, you can say, "Your teacher and I speak about you regularly, because we both care about how you are doing and it helps us do a better job of parenting and teaching."

How To Handle Negative Reports From School

When you receive a report that your child has exhibited poor performance at school, consider using consequences at home. However, a child's poor behavior at school often indicates the child's need for more structure at home, more intimate bonding with one or more of his parents, more of a feeling of control over his own life, or any combination of these.

Using Negative Consequences At Home

If you elect to try using negative consequences at home for this problem, inform your child that she must behave well in school to preserve her privileges at home. Adopt the 1-2-3 Warning System to the situation by instituting the following rule: On her third negative behavior report from school, she loses one of her privileges for a set period of time.

Allowing Your Child To Experience "Failure"

By the time your child reaches the age of eight or nine, and certainly by the time he reaches his twelfth year, you may have better results improving his school performance by allowing him to experience the natural consequences of his actions rather than by imposing consequences. Let your child experience the disappointment of a low test score, the feeling of not having an assignment done on time, the discomfort of a detention. Wait for him to realize that he has responsibility for doing his work and behaving well in school. Show your child that you will not rescue him from the problems he brings upon himself through irresponsible actions.

Avoid Inciting Rebellion

If the consequences your child brings upon herself at school and instituting consequences for school performance at home do not prove sufficient to motivate better efforts in school, consider the possibility that your behavior toward your child at home may be inciting her rebellion at school. When a child feels her parents care more about her behavior or performance than they care about her, the child feels driven to do even worse as a form of retaliation.

Avoid inciting your child's rebellion by showing her that you care about her and that you sympathize with any difficulty she has in life. Eliminate overbearing behavior you may have been exhibiting, and take time to hear your child's side in all things. This shows your child that you believe in her.

Skills

School behavior problems often stem from a child's weakness in academic skills. Instead of automatically assuming your child's behavior to be the problem, provide your child with some form of tutorial assistance. Tutoring companies provide this service as do private tutors. Be sure to focus the help your child receives on developing your child's fundamental academic skills. I have seen "miracles" take place in a child's behavior at school when the child received the help he needed for academic skill development.

Home Discipline

School discipline problems almost always point to problematic in your child's home environment or life. As you provide your child your child with the love, structure and attention she needs at home, her behavior outside the home demonstrates more maturity. If a school behavior problem exists, begin working on all the elements put forth in this book.

To Encourage Good Grades

Connect the child's privileges to his grades. Insist on a B average and show him that you will, in every way necessary, offer the support he needs to achieve this (short of doing his work for him). If his grades fall below a B average, discuss the problem with the teacher and consider tutorial assistance.

Note For The Parents Of New Preschoolers

By the time your child reaches the age of two-and-a-half, he is ready to spend a few hours a day away from home in a preschool setting. If your child throws a tantrum when you drop him off, work on calming your own emotional reaction on the way home. Check in with the teacher by phone to see how your child is doing. Usually, children do fine as soon as the parent leaves. It is the moment of transition that gives children difficulty. If this is the case with your child, his tearful screams and desperate clinging during the period of separation represent no reason for concern.

In general, children have less difficulty separating from parents if their teacher greets them outside the school and then takes them from the car into the building. If that is not possible, take your child into the school and then leave him with the teacher outside the classroom. The point here is to avoid creating in the child's mind an association between the school or classroom and the experience of separation from the parent.

Your attitude toward leaving your child at preschool strongly influences your child's attitude toward the experience. If your child demonstrates strong feelings of insecurity, examine your own feelings more closely. Work on strengthening your positive attitude toward separating from your child, and your child soon will feel more positive as well.

♦

Solution #9

Homework

Unless you have specific problems in the child's homework environment, routine or relationship with you that relate specifically to his homework behavior, consider his resistance to doing homework as a school behavior and refer to the preceding section.

To help him fulfill homework responsibilities, consider the following tips that have worked well in many homes:

1. ***Do not use nagging, anger, pleading, screaming, hitting, or arguing to "make" your child do her homework.*** This wastes your energy in a power-struggle over the issue, and it teaches your child to behave similarly when she does not get her way. It also encourages your child to continue resisting your direction so she can achieve a sense of power and control derived from your stressful reaction to her irresponsible action.

2. ***Institute consequences at home for not finishing homework.*** Establish a set time and place that your child must do his homework everyday. Until he completes his assignment, his typical evening privileges that follow the homework period remain suspended. This consequence may mean that your child watches no television or videos, plays no video games, receives or makes no phone calls, or may not socialize with friends until all homework is finished.

3. ***If your child refuses to do her homework, do not react.***
Use Conscious Detachment so she does not receive a sense
of power, retaliation or control over you for failing to do
her homework.   You can remind her *once* of the
consequences for not doing her work.   If your child says
she does not care about the consequence, do not be
manipulated. Let her experience the negative consequences
at school and at home, and see if a change in behavior
occurs.

4. ***If she lies when she tells you she has no homework or
it is all done, issue a consequence for lying.*** If this
becomes a pattern, ask her teacher to send her home every
day with a note you must sign listing her assignments. If
she loses the note or lies when she tells you the teacher
forgot to give her one, issue a consequence. (This behavior
points to the child's serious need for basic changes at home
and/or in the way you relate with him.)

5. ***On days when your child has no homework or
studying to do, have him do a household chore during
that time or involve him in some form of home study
activity.*** This helps establish self-discipline for that time of
day and removes any incentive to fib about not having
homework.

6. ***Avoid distracting the child and keep her homework
environment orderly and quiet.*** Once distracted, it can
be hard for her to re-focus.

7. ***When you help your child with homework, be patient
and encouraging.*** Do not criticize your child or become
angry or impatient *no matter what he does.* If you react with
negativity or tension, your reaction interferes with the
educational process.

8. ***If your child dawdles, becomes distracted or wastes time while you wait to help her, use The 1-2-3 Warning System.*** Each time you have to direct your child's focus back to her homework assignments or prompt her out of dawdling, advance the count. As a consequence for reaching the count of three, do not help your child with the assignment and let her suffer the consequences in school. If she cannot complete her assignment without your help and forfeits your assistance, she also receives consequences at home for incomplete homework. This approach teaches your child to value your willingness to help.

9. ***If your child regularly struggles with schoolwork, obtain assistance for her.*** A tutor or a professional learning center may help your child develop the academic strengths and skills necessary to excel easily in school. Quite often a child resists doing schoolwork because he secretly lacks confidence in his ability or finds it so hard that he loses self-esteem.

10. ***Eliminate your use of any limiting labels or negative criticism regarding your child's intelligence or school abilities.*** If you feel disappointed in his homework, remain emotionally neutral. He may be testing you. Criticizing his work may give him an excuse to do poorly. Tell him that you believe he can do better if you believe that, but allow him to experience the teacher's response to his work if he shows no interest in doing better. (Refer to the previous section, specifically the subheading on grades.) Under no circumstances should you do the work for him.

11. ***Fill your home with books, and convey your love of learning to your child.*** Children automatically adopt the underlying drives, interests and potentials of those around them. The more you demonstrate a love of learning, study and academic interest, especially during your child's first six years, the more natural it will be for him to want to learn,

study and do well in school. Have an abundance of books on all subjects. This peaks your child's curiosity and offers him opportunities to quickly and easily pursue his interests. The fewer obstacles between your child and learning the better. Provide your child with an environment expressing a passion for study and learning, and he will express that passion in his behavior naturally.

◆

Solution #10

Encouraging Honesty

Society today teaches children, albeit in an unspoken manner, that lying is acceptable. They see this displayed on television, in movies and even by the actions of adults around them. In a more outright way, children hear people speak of certain lies as harmless and necessary; for instance, we refer to "white lies" as "kind" and "good." And yet, we tell our children, "Lying is wrong." This contradictory message confuses children tremendously.

Being Honest About Honesty

Perhaps we need to change our entire approach to the way we talk about lying and honesty to children. If we begin to confront the matter more honestly and accurately and less emotionally, we may end up creating a more honest society.

To help your child understand this difficult concept, consider using the following pointers, which have worked well for many parents:

1. *Consistently treat your child as a person of integrity who is honest and honorable.* Avoid labeling her, "Liar," even if you catch her in a lie. By holding the image of your child as an honest, descent person, you help her to build a positive self-image that supports her drive to live up to that level. Lying comes more easily and naturally to children who think of themselves as liars.

2. **When your child does lie, treat it as a misbehavior, not
    evidence of a character flaw.** Discuss the matter. You
    may administer a consequence for the lie. However, do not
    attack your child's sense of worth for his behavior. Your
    angry condemnation may lower your child's value and
    expectations of himself, resulting in strengthening his
    dishonest tendencies.

3. **If you know your child did something she was not
    supposed to do, do not ask her if she did it.** When you
    already know what your child has done, asking if she did it
    is like trying to trick her into believing that you do not
    already know the answer to your question. Such trickery
    demonstrates dishonesty on your part. Trickery teaches
    your child by example to be deceptive. Treat your child as
    you would if you expected her to be honest. If you know
    she did something, do not give her the temptation to lie her
    way out of it. If you need to confront her on the issue, tell
    her what you know. If you feel her actions warrant a
    consequence, issue one. If she denies that she did
    something you know, without a doubt, she did, simply tell
    her that you know the facts and if she does not want a
    consequence for lying she needs to not repeat the lie. Do
    not demand that she admit to her misdeed, but if she does
    admit it, thank and praise her for her straightforwardness.
    If she insists on sticking to her lie, issue an additional
    consequence for her dishonesty.

4. **If you do not know the truth, accept your child's word
    without interrogation.** You may suspect that your child
    has done something, but if you ask him and he denies it, do
    not press the issue. Demonstrate that you expect him to be
    honest and he will work harder to live up to that
    expectation. If you find out later that he lied to you,
    administer one consequence for what he did and another
    one for his attempt to cover it up with a lie.

5. ***Do not overreact to your child's mistakes.*** Children feel safer telling a lie than the truth when their parents react to their mistakes with anger and criticism that wounds their feelings and hurts their self-esteem. When parents react this way, children find honesty increasingly difficult and counter to their basic survival instincts.

6. ***Overlook harmless fantasy.*** We have been discussing lying used to by children to avoid responsibility. Another kind of lying involves children weaving fantasies for the sake of impressing others or amusing themselves.

7. ***Be honest yourself, especially <u>with</u> yourself.***

◆

Solution #11

Sibling Rivalry

Sibling rivalry occurs in both obvious and subtle ways. You can recognize it easily, for example, when your children argue with one another or tease one another. However, you may not even know it is occurring when your children employ its more subtle forms. For instance, one child may act out when you pay attention to his brother. You might think that child simply wants more of your attention when, in actuality, *he may only want to win the competition* for your attention. In other words, he does not want more attention for himself; he wants more attention than his brother receives.

Watching one sibling abuse another sibling has to be one of the hardest thing for parents to do. You want to rush in and rescue your mistreated child from his sibling, but that is not always the best response to take. Intervening might not actually stop one child from behaving harshly toward the other or aid the abused child in dealing with the situation.

If you have more than one child, you must face the fact that sibling rivalry is a fact of your life and theirs. However, you can lessen how often it occurs and to what extreme it is taken by your children. The following basic guidelines can help you:

1. ***Do not over-involve yourself in your children's interactions.*** You only have limited energy to control what happens around you. The more tired you feel, the less power you have to direct your children skillfully. Before automatically reacting to their conflicts, pause and consider

if a better option would be to overlook their behavior. Do not expect perfection in your children's way of interacting with each other.

2. *If you observe one of your children obviously behaving poorly toward the other to an extent too serious to overlook, respond with peace, poise and firmness.* Inform that child of the behavior she needs to change and begin counting for a consequence. If she complains that her behavior toward her sibling was not her fault, remind her that she is responsible for how she behaves regardless of how others behave toward her. If she argues, "That's not fair," simply refuse to discuss the matter *at that time.* If she continues to complain, ignore her or advance the count. Later, have a discussion in which you listen to and try to understand your child's perspective and in which you help her understand yours.

3. *If you do not know which child is responsible for the inappropriate behavior exhibited, simply begin counting the children as a group for a consequence.* If a child complains that he should not be blamed, advance the count for that child. If a child obviously ignores your count and continues misbehaving, advance the count for that child. One consequence that works well here is simply a Time Out from one another for a period of time.

4. *Discuss with each child positive strategies for dealing with sibling rivalry.* If the children's conflict becomes a routine problem, schedule private discussions with each child in which you explain how you want that particular child to behave toward her sibling. Listen to your child's complaints about her sibling, and help her develop acceptable strategies for dealing with the difficulties.

5. *Do not be controlled by negative behavior from one or more of your children.* When more than one of your children demonstrate a behavior you want to discourage,

such as bickering or hitting, watch your reaction. If you respond with anger or stress you teach them that mistreating each other gets you involved. Pause before reacting, and consider what you want to accomplish. Give your children a few moments to realize that manipulative behavior cannot control you. If they do not settle down on their own, calmly but firmly give them the option of either getting along better or being separated for a while. If they ignore you, begin counting them for a consequence. If one complains that you are not being fair, do not argue about it.

6. ***Separate your children when they do not get along.*** Separation proves to be an effective way to stop siblings from fighting. If they cannot get along, establish the rule that they are not permitted to sit together, to look at each other, to talk with each other, to play with each other, or to interact in any way. You can impose this for a day, a week or even longer. In many cases, the children soon begin to miss each other and start interacting positively. Problems between siblings often arise because they have been spending too much time together.

7. ***Create order out of chaos and peace out of strife.*** Avoid reacting to your children's battles with anger, hitting, screaming, or pleading, because when you behave in these ways you add to the chaos. Respond to your children's disturbing battles or wildness with the peace and poise you want them to exhibit. (See The Law Of Reflection)

8. ***Let your children learn from the consequences they bring upon themselves.*** Allow your children to work out their own problems with each other. If one does something to annoy the other, let the other's response teach him through the consequences of his reaction. This permits your children to learn and to develop their relationship skills through their experience of the relationship.

9. ***Stay out of your children's disputes as much as possible.*** Do not fall into the automatic, habitual pattern of becoming absorbed in their conflicts. You become part of the problem by involving yourself unnecessarily. Withdraw yourself when their interactions become ugly or obnoxious. This teaches your children that they need to get along to keep you involved.

10. ***Discourage "tattling" by encouraging the "tattler" to handle on his own the problem about which he is complaining.*** If the tattler starts to nag or whine in an attempt to get you involved, start counting the tattler or simply use Conscious Detachment.

11. ***Sometimes siblings appear to be fighting against one another when they actually are joining forces against the parents.*** Discourage this scenario by restraining yourself from reacting to their rivalries with visible annoyance. Remain emotionally poised, and observe what happens. Often, just by staying calm and showing them that you are aware of their behavior, the children choose a better way of behaving.

12. ***Make a Bill of Rights.*** Define in writing the ways in which the members of your family are to behave toward one another. State the behaviors you want and do not want as "We do..." and "We do not..." For instance, "We speak kindly to one another" and "We do not use foul language, hitting or yelling." Have each member of the household sign the document, and then give each a copy. When your children demonstrate compliance with the rules for relating as written in your family bill of rights, praise and thank them. If they like stickers, turn the list into a daily chart. They receive a star for each positive way of relating with each other that they demonstrated each day.

◆

Solution #12

Money and Allowance

As with anything else, help your child develop a practical approach to money by demonstrating that attitude yourself. Even though it may not be apparent, your child automatically adopts your values. If you have personal tendencies that limit your ability to handle money well or to attract it in abundance, your child accepts those limiting tendencies into his personality (see Chapter on "The Law Of Reflection").

Take a good look at your attitude toward and management of money. Start educating yourself about finances. Look at your parents' attitude toward money, and see how it has affected you. As you become more aware of your own relationship with money you can raise your level of functioning in this area, thereby giving your child more enlightened or influences.

You can further help your child develop a practical knowledge of money, which constitutes a part of his necessary preparations for life, by following these guidelines:

1. ***Begin giving your child an allowance by the time he reaches the age of two or three.*** This early acquaintance with money helps your child develop comfort and confidence in money and his ability to handle it. He may not understand the concept of money immediately, but he will develop an understanding of personal economics and confidence in his economic independence sooner than if he does not experience having his own money.

2. *The amount of allowance to give your child depends upon your own budget and upon the things for which she might need money during the week.*

3. *Teach your child financial responsibility.* Explain the concepts of savings and investments, as well as the concept of "compound interest." Teach him to set aside 10 percent of his allowance for savings, 10 percent for investments and 10 percent for charity. This gets him into the habit of spending no more than 70 percent of the money he receives. When he wants a candy bar at the grocery store, or a new toy he sees on the toy store shelf, tell him the cost and ask him if he has enough money to make the purchase. If he does not have the full amount with him, you can loan him the money if you choose. If he does not have enough in savings to cover the cost, tell him that he needs to save his money to purchase it at a later date. You can advance your child the money for what he desires occasionally, but never advance him more than a portion of the following week's allowance. If he wants to save for something in particular, discuss how long it will take for him to accumulate enough to make the purchase. You can help him create a written record of his savings with the target amount written as a goal, so he can visualize his progress. Saving for a larger purchase teaches your child patience and self-control. Introduce your child to the mathematical process you go through in determining how long it will take to save the necessary amount of money. If your child wants to spend money impetuously, do not rescue him from this act. Let him spend the money and then experience the natural consequence of not being able to purchase the item for which he has been saving.

4. ***Do not set up allowance as payment for doing chores.***
   Chores represent your child's contribution to the home and
   family. If she neglects her chores, however, you can
   deduct a portion of her allowance as a consequence. While
   this might seem to imply that she receives payment for
   chores, it really does not. Remember, allowance represents
   a privilege just like any other. You can take away any
   privilege you choose for incomplete or undone chores.

5. ***You can pay bonuses for special contributions to the
   family and home.*** While promising your child a reward
   for appropriate behavior is not recommended, offering
   your child a special reward for an extra chore or service that
   he contributes can work well. For instance, if washing your
   car is not one of your child's regular chores and he offers to
   do so for some extra cash, you can certainly accept his
   offer.

6. ***From the age of two or three, involve your child in
   monetary interactions with clerks and servers.*** Let the
   child hand the clerk the money and receive the change.
   When she is old enough, let her count the change to make
   sure it is all there. Before your child is able to count the
   change on her own, let her see you counting it -- or, better
   still, count it with her. If you have to write a check, as soon
   as she is able let her write it and present it to you for your
   signature. This not only involves your child in constructive
   activity (avoiding misbehavior that occurs when she has
   nothing to do), it helps her feel like a responsible part of the
   world and gives her a sense of contribution and
   competence -- all of which boost your child's healthy self-
   confidence and self-esteem.

7. ***Allow your teen to benefit from having a job in the "real world."*** A job provides teenagers with the practical experience and independence from their parents that they crave while, at the same time, cultivating positive work skills and habits. Traditional school settings do not satisfy your teen's deeper yearning for the real-life experience that work in the world provides. When your teen begins earning his own money, you no longer need to give him an allowance. He will gain a great deal of satisfaction and self-worth from "taking home a pay check" and spending money he has earned from a "real" job.

◆

Solution #13

Children And Pets

Children usually love animals instinctively. A child's heart opens to the incredible sweetness and innocence in pets, a much similar reaction to that which takes place in adults observing happy children.

Compassion drives children to want to interact with nature's creatures, and by allowing and even encouraging them to do so we support their compassionate development. If we oppose a child's natural instinct for contact with the animal kingdom, we run the risk of creating an inhibiting pattern within the child that limits true self-expression.

Providing your child with a pet supplies the opportunity to feel and to express love. It expands your child's level of companionship and enlarges her sense of family and home.

A happy, healthy pet increases peace and contentment in the home. However, an unhappy, poorly cared for pet experiences stress that, in turn, increases tensions in the home. Before you bring a pet home, be sure it will have the environment, attention and general care it needs to be happy and healthy.

When a pet enters your home, it comes into a kind of hierarchy with its place below that of your child. This means that if your child feels bullied by a parent, your child will bully the pet. You can tell how your child feels about the treatment he receives by observing how he treats his pet.

Teach children under six how to care for pets through demonstration. Do not simply tell your child to touch the cat gently. Consistently show her the exact physical movements you want her to use.

If your child is under six years of age and plays too roughly or touches his pet in a dangerous, hurtful or annoying manner, remind him, "You must be gentle with your pet or you cannot play with it." Then immediately guide your child away from the pet or protect the pet by placing it somewhere away from your child. Separating your child from the pet acts as a kind of Time Out, teaching him that he has to treat the pet well to have the privilege of interacting with the pet. If you hit your child or hurt your child's feelings through verbal attack in reaction to his mistreatment of the pet, your child may resent the pet because he feels it is the pet's fault he was punished. This may result in your child's treatment of the pet worsening rather than improving.

Owning a pet gives your child the chance to practice caring for someone other than herself. By the time a child reaches the age of three, she can assume responsibility for feeding and watering, as well as cleaning the bowls, cage or litter box of her pet. Place within the child's easy reach the items she needs to perform these functions, and show your child the exact steps to follow when performing these tasks.

Before you bring a pet into your child's life, be sure you have the time, energy and motivation to care for the pet yourself. If you do not have this, you probably should not acquire a pet. Although pets can enrich family life, if you are not prepared to care for the animal in the event that your child proves to be an unreliable caretaker, the result may be more family strife and tension. Plus, the pet will suffer considerably.

Lessons Of Life And Death

In the event that your child's pet dies, treat the matter with solemnity. Have some kind of funeral ceremony to enhance the child's respect for life and death and to help the child through this difficult period. Do not become harsh or impatient with your child's grieving process. After about a month, begin a quest for a new pet. This teaches your child that feelings of loss need not be a fixed or permanent emotion, and it builds the child's trust in something good following periods of difficulty and pain.

◆

Introduction To Solutions #14 - 18

Living, Loving Relationship Solutions

The following solutions apply the principles of *Parenting With Love* to aspects of your life that indirectly, but deeply, impact your child's self-esteem and behavior. As you improve your functioning in these areas, you support your child's development in crucial ways. All the following solutions may not pertain to your particular situation. Feel free to read only those that prove relevant for you and your child.

Each of these issues addressed deserves an entire book devoted specifically to how they relate to your child. Therefore, regard the following as basic pointers aiming your efforts in directions that can both improve your child's behavior and enrich your child's life.

♦

Solution #14

Marriage With Love

Children need their parents to have a strong, harmonious relationship that has already endured some difficult trials before their arrival on the scene. The presence of a child burdens the weakest links in a relationship. Therefore, establish a strong, loving, respectful relationship with your spouse *before* you have children, and be prepared to continue working hard to keep the relationship growing in love when you have children.

In general, how you relate to people teaches your child how to relate to others. More specifically, the way in which you and your spouse interact profoundly impacts how your child learns to interact in intimate relationships.

Children's behavior often reflects the state of their parents' marriage. When you and your spouse exhibit stressful conflict and unhappiness, your child feels disturbed and responds with disturbing behavior.

You express your feelings toward your spouse constantly. You cannot hide your feelings. Children exhibit more sensitivity than adults. Thus, they feel the hurt of any critical, angry, impatient feeling you experience, even though you may deny that feeling to yourself. Relating insensitively or disrespectfully with your spouse results in your child feeling badly about you. Your child will also feel badly about himself because children blame themselves for how their parents interact. Telling your child that he bares no responsibility for your marital problems does not solve the problem. Telling him that no real marital problems exist, when he can feel that they do, causes him to seriously doubt himself. Any form of abuse between spouses victimizes the child.

The place to begin solving your marital problems is within yourself. Come to terms with your true feelings by allowing yourself to openly and honestly feel what you feel. Most, if not all, serious marital difficulties stem from early childhood needs that went unmet. As you face and resolve your early childhood issues with your own parents, you can come to terms with your needs in your marriage.

The foundation of a loving marriage lies in the commitment to making and keeping it a loving marriage. Just being committed to preserving the relationship is not enough. For the sake of yourself, your spouse *and your children*, commit to preserving and building upon the love between yourself and your spouse.

◆

Solution #15

Divorcing With Love

Children grieve over their parents' divorce far more deeply than most adults realize (or want to admit to themselves). They suffer profound emotional conflict and mental confusion about the break-up of the family, and they often feel responsible. This sense of personal responsibility leads to feelings of low self-esteem or even destructive self-hatred for the child.

Be patient with and tolerant of your child's feelings as she moves, like you, through the stages of the divorce process. Your child needs a safe place to express the painful emotions she feels. Supply her with ample opportunities to express and to feel her feelings without blame, shame or criticism.

Divorce brings major transition into a child's life; and transitions disturb the orderly patterns of a child's behavior. Understand that your child's behavior may fall to a lower level during the early stages of her divorce experience. However, she still needs boundaries and rules clearly established and consistently upheld. Studies have shown that children suffer more from the lax parenting they receive while their parents move through the stages of divorce than from the divorce itself.

Be more careful than ever to avoid using harsh criticism, anger, yelling or hitting when your child's behavior disappoints you. Use calm and kind conversation (if she has the maturity to understand at this level) to clarify that you still uphold the rules for her behavior for her own good. Back up the rules with the kind of consequence systems you have learned in this book.

One important point to keep in mind pertains to your ongoing relationship with your former spouse. If you maintain a critical, angry, condescending attitude toward your child's other parent, you place the child in a very painful position. To feel loved and accepted by you, the child feels forced to deny the positive feelings she may have toward her other parent. In addition, on some level she probably resents you out of loyalty to her other parent.

Reject the common opinion that tells you that divorce must be destructive. Assuming the divorce was truly necessary, if moved through properly, everyone involved can emerge better off as a result of this step. Grief over loss will occur, but such grieving over what was lost proves far more beneficial than living in denial of what truly was a destructive relationship. While the family must adjust to the major transition, the divorce can create a healthier, more stable and more supportive family structure for everyone now that the child's parents have found the kind of relationship that works best for all concerned.

◆

Solution #16

Single Parenting With Love

The single greatest challenge for single parents involves learning to manage both their time and energy effectively. If you work full-time, which most single parents are forced to do, you may experience the strain of overwhelm and overload on a daily basis. Many single parents experience loneliness as well, since time and energy constraints make it seem that they have no free time or energy to find or create a new intimate relationship.

The way to move through problems successfully begins with addressing them clearly, accurately and honestly. Your needs can be met, but you must first discover them for yourself. From there, make a list of things you need in your life and begin planning and organizing your time to address those needs in the order of their importance. If you look at your daily life closely, you will recognize at least small opportunities to prepare for what you want in your life; and you will find at least small steps you can take to advance in the direction you want your life to take.

Single parents, as well as married parents experiencing marital trouble, make a common error when they become emotionally dependent upon their children. For example, without realizing it, you may expect your teenager to help you in ways you would normally expect your spouse to help. You might rely on your young child for emotional or affectionate nurturing when those needs should be net by yourself or another adult.

Emotional dependency upon children of any age proves seriously damaging to their self-esteem and to their sense of real and appropriate boundaries. This dependency hurts their self-esteem because they never feel truly adequate at performing the task you have given them. It blurs their sense of appropriate boundaries because when you develop a parent-child dependency in your relationship, your child becomes confused about intimacy issues. This makes that child more vulnerable to destructive intimate relationships later in life and usually generates deep feelings of resentment, fear and helplessness in your child that can take a long time and a lot of effort to repair.

◆

Solution #17

Step Parenting With Love

The step parent enters a family at a distinct disadvantage, automatically perceived by the stepchild as an intruder and as a threat to life as he knows it as well as to his relationship with his biological parents. This problem is compounded when one of the biological parents feels threatened by or jealous of the stepparent and encourages the child to distrust and to dislike that person.

As a step parent, accept the fact that you cannot rush or force a positive relationship with your step child. Drop any expectations you have of becoming instantly close to your step child or of her automatically treating you with parental respect and affection. Even with no interference by the biological parent, it may take a number of years to actually develop the kind of relationship you want to have with your step child.

You can build the positive, trusting, and loving relationship you want with your step child by:

1. Insuring that your relationship with your new spouse continues to grow in love, respect and honesty.

2. Patiently and persistently working on understanding yourself, your step child and the relationship dynamics between the two of you.

Do not blame your step child for your feelings of frustration or inadequacy when the relationship you want with him does not bloom as quickly as you would like. You have to work long and hard and with true humility to overcome the natural obstacles to the success of your relationship. Your commitment to your own personal growth process, to accepting and loving the child unconditionally just as he is and to the true love in your marriage will serve as the fundamental requirement for effective step parenting.

♦

Solution #18

Dealing With Grandparents With Love

Your parents or in-laws may offer what they believe to be well-meaning advice, but only you and your spouse have the ultimate responsibility for the parenting your child receives. Another opinion serves as no adequate substitute for your own inner sense of right and wrong for your child. If your child's grandparents impose their advice to the point that it interferes with your effectiveness as a parent, tell them privately, in a kind but firm manner, that they need to stop interfering. If they insist on relating to your child in ways that you regard as improper or unhealthy for your child, clearly inform them again that this must stop. If this request falls on deaf ears, you need to limit their access to you or to your children. In all decisions relating to the welfare of your child, your child's well-being must come ahead of the grandparents' wishes.

◆

EPILOGUE

Beyond Discipline

Child discipline systems or methods of any kind fail as long as the adults using them deny their own undisciplined, unbalanced, irresponsible behavior patterns. You cannot "fix" children who live in a broken society with broken parents and broken teachers. The values and behaviors of today's children mirror precisely the way those around them live and relate.

We usually think of child discipline problems as entirely the child's fault. However, child behavior is largely a product of the treatment and influences a child receives. By providing a child with the elements he needs for more responsible, cooperative, positive behavior, we diminish our need to deal with problematic child behavior. As you follow your life's path toward your own highest values, your child receives the structure, function and order he needs to develop healthy and happy self-discipline.

Focus more on prevention of behavior problems than on the cure for misbehavior. Think more about what your child needs from you to behave well, to feel good about herself, to develop true strength of character than about what you want from your child.

The Child's World

As long as we perpetuate confused and chaotic social environments for our children we provide children with influences that work counter to the behavior and values we want from them. For example, every time your teen hears a politician make a biased, intentionally ambiguous speech he learns to lie.   Every time your 10-year-old sees adults demonstrating morally corrupt or psychologically unbalanced behavior, her moral and psychological behavior patterns shift to be more in line with this model.   Every time your three-year-old watches television and sees one cartoon character hit another, he unconsciously notes that hitting -- or violence in general -- is an appropriate way to relate with others.

We have to clean the dirt off the streets if we expect children to honor cleanliness, and we have to honor the sacredness in every human being to bring out our children's potential for compassion and respectfulness.   The lowest element of society merely reflects the lowest element in ourselves.   Condemning those who demonstrate moral corruption veils the elements of our own moral weakness but does not eliminate it.   The lies at all levels of business, education and government have to be replaced with more accurate representations of the truth to teach our children respect for truth.   To support children in following the right paths and living in the right ways, neighborhoods need neighbors who treat one another with respect, charity and trust.

Repair Yourself To Help Repair Society

Blaming others or the society in which children are raised does not help the situation in your home or with your child.   In fact, angry, self-righteous tirades of negative judgment projected upon others teaches your child to excuse her own negativity.

You do not have to feel overwhelmed by all the problems in our society and by how they affect your child. Instead, you can focus on making natural, patient improvements in your own values and conduct.   Honestly "repairing" ourselves provides a societal basis that supports the goals we have for our children. For your children's best development, you have to slow down, calm down and take the time you need to live more consciously, to make better choices, to live with more intelligence and to love *yourself.*

Everything we perceive as wrong with the world today, we create and re-create everyday with the choices we make. These choices hurt children and make parenting and teaching them more difficult than need be. Everyone wants everyone else to fix the problem. Everyone else thinks someone else caused the problem. This teaches children to blame the world -- or, at least, someone else -- for their problems instead of working on themselves. Make the world a better place by showing your child how to make better choices that create better behaviors, self-images and better lives. Show your child how to do this by modeling the same behavior. Order, cleanliness, peace, and respectful relationships will not come from children in abundance until those elements come to children in abundance.

The Place Of Child Discipline Systems

You cannot wait for the world to change to help your child. While understanding that negative influences exists that remain out of your control, you still can use a child discipline system consciously and compassionately to produce better results with your children.

The child discipline system you have learned in this book can be reduced to eight simple steps:

1. ***Practice maintaining your own emotional balance and harmony, then parent with compassion and love.*** As long as you react to your child's behavior with anger, stress, yelling, pleading, nagging, arguing, or hitting your child's behavior dominates you. You also teach your child to behave in the same negative manner.

2. *Use the 1-2-3 Warning System consistently.* This teaches your child to respond to warnings and gives her the chance to discipline herself.

3. *Restrict your child's privileges or the unnecessary things you do to please him when he behaves in disrespectful, non-cooperative ways.*

4. *Do not try to control everything.* If you exhaust yourself by working too hard to be in control your parenting skills and capacity to enjoy your children suffer. You can only control or change so much so quickly; the rest you must learn to trust and let go.

5. *Respect BOTH your child's and your own will and feelings.* Show your child compassionate respect for her feelings and will no matter how irrational they may seem, but also respect your feelings and what you want. Keep a balance here and you teach your child to respect herself and others.

6. *Do not waste one ounce of your energy or time in saying or doing anything in an effort to control your child that does not work.* Draining, straining or humiliating yourself, involving yourself in power struggles, pointlessly arguing, or endlessly explaining serve neither you nor the child.

7. *Step back and strategize before reacting.* Hasty, emotional reactions to problems usually create more chaos. Be gentle and respectful toward yourself by giving yourself time to calmly consider the situation, your options and your objectives *before* responding.

8. *Your unconditional love provides your child with the foundation of self-worth he needs to make truly good choices in life.* He will discipline himself as he learns that he is worthy of good treatment.

"Lucky" Parenting

A happy, well-behaved child does not happen by magic or luck. Child discipline problems usually indicate a family-living-situation to which the child is doing her best to adjust. Bringing a child into unstable, inharmonious conditions, raising her without clear, firm and reasonable boundaries consistently upheld, or relating with her in such a way that her real feelings and true self go unrecognized, disrespected or rejected, virtually guarantees some kind of child behavior problem.

Even with ideal parenting, children undergo the destructive influences of our unbalanced society with its contradictory, superficial and deranged values. Yet, by honestly doing your best in parenting, you can do much to prepare your child to live in and enjoy the grand adventure of moving through this scared, yet sometimes confusing world.

Many parents do not read parenting books because, while the methods and theories may make perfect sense, they remain unhelpful and inadequate. The parents know deep down inside, either consciously or unconsciously, that the problems they have with their children stem from some core issues within themselves. For instance, only as the parent builds more balance, security and trust in his ways of relating with the child does his child automatically adopt and express more of the qualities in his own attitude and behavior.

Serving The Child

A wonderful teacher used to say to me, "Your luck is your look. Good look." By this he meant that my look, my alertly aware attentiveness, offers me the key to unlock the opportunities which are always present. You have opportunities for truly serving your child every moment.

We usually think of child discipline in the sense of controlling the child. However, controlling the child may not be in the child's best interest nor improve his behavior. When you seek to control your child to please yourself, you set up the conditions for a power struggle between you and your child, each wanting his own way with the other. The essence of loving child discipline expresses in serving the child: setting limits for the sake of the child's truly sound and healthy development, based on the child's true needs.

Serving your child begins with *observing* your child. Each of your children, at each moment, expresses a unique need. Your ability to serve your child grows out of your ability to really know and recognize your own needs, and to respect yourself enough to meet those needs.

I trust this book has offered you some insight into ways of better meeting your child's and your own true needs with love. May your home be blessed with peace, love and the light of parenting solutions that truly work.

◆

"We do not need to be told
whether to be strict or permissive
with our children.
What we do need is to have respect for
their needs, their feelings,
and
their individuality,
as well as for our own."

- Dr. Alice Miller

◆

About
<u>BOB LANCER</u>

Child discipline specialist Bob Lancer is a dynamic, motivational teacher and speaker, as well as a talk radio host, television personality, author and consultant. His ability to inspire and empower parents to bring their very best into their relationship with their children contributes to the uniqueness of his penetrating message and presentation style. Since 1994, he has presented his leading-edge approach to child discipline for *today's* world through his **Take Charge Now!** Workshops and talks to thousands of parents in Atlanta, Georgia. He currently hosts his own popular talk radio shows, appears weekly on local television, and has been interviewed on CNN as a child discipline expert.

He has been referred to as "The most dynamic and moving spokesperson on parenting issues and the true needs of the child," and "The guru of parent temper control." To date, he has produced a wealth of enlightening and inspiring audio tapes on parenting, and he has authored an illustrated, humorous, motivational book of stories for young children, entitled *The Longtime Tales of Uncle Mo.*

His work has been enthusiastically endorsed by professionals in the fields of Psychology, Social Service, Pediatrics and Education. He holds a degree in Education and has done post-graduate work in Counseling Psychology and Educational Technology, and taught school for a number of years.

You can order a free catalogue of Bob Lancer's
work by writing to:
Parenting Solutions
P.O. Box 70031
Marietta, GA 30007

◆

A SELECTION OF BOOKS AND RECORDINGS BY BOB LANCER AVAILABLE THROUGH PARENTING SOLUTIONS PUBLISHING

1. _THE DIRECT YOUR LIFE PROCESS_
Simply keys for balancing and directing your life (Cassette: $9.95)

2. _LIGHTEN UP!_
How to harness the power of happiness to create the life you want
(Book: $9.95)

3. _PARENTING WITH LOVE, Without Anger or Stress_
Breakthrough book on conscious parenting: How to sucessfully guide your
child's behavior without anger or stress ($15.95)

4. _THE LONGTIME TALES OF UNCLE MO_
Motivational, illustrated story-book for children inspiring them to fulfill their
higher potential with compassion. Fosters literacy. ($9.95)

5. _RAISING SELF ESTEEM_
Stop beating yourself up and start lifting yourself up! (Cassette: $9.95)

6. _WHAT TO DO ABOUT YOUR THINKING_
How to release yourself from self-imposed mind-limits (Cassette: $9.95)

7. _SOULMATE LESSONS_
How to find the relationship that's right for you and avoid destructive
relationships. (Cassette: $9.95)

8. _YOUR VICTORIOUS SELF_
How to turn every experience into a win, including loss (Cassette: $9.95)

9. _OVERCOMING YOUR PARENTS' LIMITING PATTERNS_
How to recognize and rise above limiting influences received in your
upbringing (cassette: $9.95)

10. _COUPLES' KEYS TO HARMONY_
Simple, powerful steps to improve peace, harmony, communication, trust,
intimacy and loving cooperation (Cassette: $9.95)

11. _THE CHILD DISCIPLINE PROCESS_
_Practical guidelines for achieving loving child-discipline using 3 simple options
without anger or stress. (Cassette: $9.95)_

12. _SPIRITUAL PARENTING_
_Approaching parenting as a spiritual path while raising
your chile to follow a higher path in life. (Cassette: $9.95)_

(To order, add $2 p/h per item and send to
Parenting Solutions / P.O. Box 70031 / Marietta, GA 30007
or email: blparents@aol.com)